Orthodox Christianity: A Very Short Introduction

VERY SHORT INTRODUCTIONS are for anyone wanting a stimulating and accessible way into a new subject. They are written by experts, and have been translated into more than 45 different languages.

The series began in 1995, and now covers a wide variety of topics in every discipline. The VSI library currently contains over 550 volumes—a Very Short Introduction to everything from Psychology and Philosophy of Science to American History and Relativity—and continues to grow in every subject area.

Very Short Introductions available now:

Available soon:

For more information visit our website

www.oup.com/vsi/

A. Edward Siecienski

ORTHODOX CHRISTIANITY

A Very Short Introduction

OXFORD
UNIVERSITY PRESS

OXFORD
UNIVERSITY PRESS

Oxford University Press is a department of the University of Oxford.
It furthers the University's objective of excellence in research, scholarship,
and education by publishing worldwide. Oxford is a registered trade mark of
Oxford University Press in the UK and certain other countries.

Published in the United States of America by Oxford University Press
198 Madison Avenue, New York, NY 10016, United States of America.

© Oxford University Press 2019

Library of Congress Cataloging-in-Publication Data
Names: Siecienski, A. Edward (Anthony Edward), author.
Title: Orthodox Christianity : a very short introduction /
A. Edward Siecienski.
Description: New York, NY : Oxford University Press, 2019. | Series: Very
short introductions | Includes bibliographical references and index.
Identifiers: LCCN 2018058956 (print) | LCCN 2019012782 (ebook) |
ISBN 9780190883287 (updf) | ISBN 9780190883294 (epub) |
ISBN 9780190883270 (pbk. : alk. paper)
Subjects: LCSH: Orthodox Eastern Church—History. |
Orthodox Eastern Church—Doctrines.
Classification: LCC BX290 (ebook) | LCC BX290 .S443 2019 (print) |
DDC 281.9—dc23
LC record available at https://lccn.loc.gov/2018058956

1 3 5 7 9 8 6 4 2

Printed in Great Britain
by Ashford Colour Press Ltd., Gosport, Hants.
on acid-free paper

Contents

Acknowledgments

This short introduction to Orthodox Christianity would not have been possible without the assistance of many friends, colleagues, and family members, all of whom provided invaluable help in its composition. Among the first to read and comment on the early drafts were my father, Edward A. Siecienski, and my dear friend, Stacy Germano. The parishioners of the Orthodox Church of the Holy Cross in Medford, New Jersey, many of whom read drafts of the book as part of an adult education class, also gave me excellent feedback and suggested several changes that I incorporated in the final version. My friends and colleagues, Drs. George Demacopoulos of Fordham University and Michael Azar of Scranton University, read portions of the manuscript and made invaluable suggestions, especially regarding Orthodoxy in the Middle East and the modern world. My wife, Kiev, and children, Alex and Alana, deserve recognition for their infinite patience as I locked myself away writing for days at a time. Finally, I would like to thank all those, from the priests and teachers of my youth to my graduate school professors, who taught me about the faith. To them, and to all who carry on this vital work, this book is humbly dedicated.

Introduction

Although it is the world's second largest Christian denomination, with somewhere between 250 and 300 million adherents, Orthodoxy remains a little known and "mysterious" entity in the West, even to those who are familiar with it. In fact, it is often the "mystical" and "exotic" nature of Orthodox Christianity that potential converts cite as its most attractive feature; to many, the unfamiliar vestments, incense, and chanting somehow make Orthodoxy seem more spiritual than Western-style worship. For others, what sticks out about Orthodoxy is its "foreignness." In the English-speaking world, many people simply assume that Orthodox Christians are all Greeks, Russians, Slavs, or Arabs, the implication being that Orthodoxy is the faith of a faraway people, brought to the West by immigrants and now embraced solely by their children.

On one level these caricatures contain some element of truth. Today most of the world's Orthodox live in Russia, Eastern Europe, and Greece, with sizable communities in Egypt, Syria, Ethiopia, Lebanon, and the Holy Land. By contrast, in the United States, Orthodox Christians account for only 0.5 percent of the total US population, more than 60 percent of whom are either first- or second-generation immigrants. Because many of these immigrants maintained links with their mother churches back home, the parishes they established in the United States were often led by priests and bishops associated with those mother churches. Thus, the United States is home to Greek Orthodox parishes, Russian Orthodox parishes, and more, many of which believe that the preservation of their national and cultural identities is an integral part of their mission.

Of course, to the Orthodox themselves, their faith is anything but "foreign." For them Orthodoxy is simply a way of being Christian that is ultimately rooted in the person of Jesus and the experience of the early church. It is literally "the correct belief," or "the correct worship" (from the Greek *orthos* and *doxa*) of God in the one true church established by his Son. Granted, its expression may vary somewhat depending on the location—for example, Russian and Greek chant sound quite different—but ultimately the Orthodox believer is convinced that s/he shares the same faith as the first generation of Christians. The expressions "That's what we've always believed" or "That's the way we've always done it" might sound at first like a petrified traditionalism, but the Orthodox have never seen it that way. Instead they hold that in their adherence to the ancient ways they are simply part of the church's "Living Tradition"—that is, celebrating the faith of those who have come before so that it can be handed on uncorrupted to those who are to come.

If the Orthodox claim to have preserved the Christian faith uncorrupted throughout the centuries, it must be recognized that there are others, particularly Roman Catholic and Protestant Christians, who make similar claims for themselves. These Christians, coming out of a Western European background and far more familiar in the English-speaking world, do indeed share centuries of history with the Orthodox. For over a millennium there was, for the most part, only one church (leaving aside, for the moment, various heretical sects and the non-Chalcedonians), and while there existed differences in language, culture, and religious practice, the Greek-speaking East and Latin-speaking West long recognized each other as members of the same family.

But when, after centuries of growing tension, a division (or "schism") arose at some point between the eleventh and thirteenth centuries, the two halves of Christianity began developing along separate trajectories. From the Orthodox perspective the matter was simple: The Latin-speaking West had embraced positions that were not in keeping with the ancient faith, and so it could no longer be recognized as belonging to the same church. Rome and the West had essentially "broken away," and while hope for restored relations continued for centuries after the break, Catholicism and, following the Reformation in 1517, Protestantism, were no longer seen as "Orthodox."

Among the difficulties for modern Orthodoxy is that the lack of any universal head—there is no Orthodox "pope"—often prevents it from presenting itself to the world as a united entity. Although they are joined together by the same faith, the Orthodox are jurisdictionally organized into fourteen (or sixteen, if one counts the Orthodox Church of America [OCA] and Ukrainian Orthodox Church) self-governing ("autocephalous") churches, most drawn along national lines and each headed by a patriarch or metropolitan bishop. While the Patriarch of Constantinople (also known as the Ecumenical Patriarch) enjoys a certain preeminence among the bishops, even he does not have the authority to speak on their behalf or command them to action. As a result, disputes among the various jurisdictions are commonplace, and efforts at coming together to deal with issues of mutual interest have all fallen horribly short. For example, the attempt in 2016 to hold a "Great and Holy Council" was hampered by the nonattendance of several churches and the outright refusal of others to subscribe to its decisions. Although theoretically Orthodoxy is supposed to be a "communion of local churches united in love," in practice it more often resembles a dysfunctional family squabbling over Christmas dinner.

In spite of these difficulties Orthodox Christianity continues to thrive, both in its traditional homelands and in the West.

Orthodoxy has played an increasingly visible role in world affairs, with the Patriarch of Moscow serving as an influential figure in shaping post-Soviet Russia and the Ecumenical Patriarch becoming a leading voice on behalf of both refugees and the environment. Recent popes have been particularly keen to improve relations with the Orthodox, seeing them not only as sharers of the same ancient faith, but also as potential partners in the battles against secularization and the persecution of Christians in the Holy Land. Although often referred to as "Eastern Christians," today there are sizable Orthodox communities in North America, Western Europe, and Oceania, where universities and centers of theological study have benefited from an increased Orthodox presence. For the Orthodox, their faith is not merely a window into Christianity's past—it is a way of keeping that past very much alive today.

Chapter 1
"In the beginning"

Ask Orthodox Christians about the "founder" of their church and they will tell you that it was founded by Christ himself some two thousand years ago and that modern-day Orthodoxy is simply the continuation of the one true church Jesus established when he was on earth. Jesus, himself a Jew "born of a woman, born under the law" (Gal. 4:4), had preached during his life about the coming of God's kingdom and the Father's desire that "the lost sheep" (Luke 15:3–7) should repent and be forgiven. This ministry of preaching and healing came to a seemingly disastrous end when Jesus was brought before the Roman authorities and crucified, dying on a cross outside the walls of Jerusalem. Yet three days later, when some women went to the tomb to anoint his body, they discovered he was not there, and an angel proclaimed to them that "he has been raised as he said" (Matt. 28:6). What at first looked like a crushing defeat for the mission of Jesus had now become its greatest victory.

Because Jesus had wanted his mission to continue, during his earthly life he gathered about him men and women who would continue to preach the gospel (a translation of the Greek *evangelion*, or "good news") following his death and ascension to the right hand of God. Twelve of these men, among whom Simon Peter had a special place, formed the foundation of this group, and it was to these "apostles" (from the Greek, meaning "one who is sent out") that leadership of the church was entrusted in the days following the resurrection. Fifty days after Jesus rose from the dead, on a day today celebrated as the Feast of Pentecost, the Holy Spirit came upon the apostles and empowered them to go out and spread the word—Jesus was the promised "Christ" ("messiah" or "anointed one") whom God had raised from the dead, and through faith in him one could conquer death itself and enjoy life eternal.

Initially there was a lot of resistance to this message, first from the Jewish authorities who believed that these followers of Jesus, now called "Christians," were guilty of blasphemy. They persecuted this small sect, creating witnesses (or "martyrs") for the faith, the first of whom was a young man named Stephen. According to the Acts of the Apostles, among those who witnessed this event was a Pharisee named Saul (better known as Paul), who "breathing threats and murder against the disciples of the Lord" went to Damascus so "that if he found any who belonged to the Way, men or women, he might bring them bound to Jerusalem" (Acts 9:1–2). Knocked off his horse by a vision of the risen Lord, Paul soon became a Christian and one of the leaders of the nascent movement. Together with the other apostles he spread the faith beyond the confines of Jerusalem and throughout the Mediterranean, bringing into the church not only Jews but also non-Jewish Greeks, who became an important part of the movement. As the faith spread, the Roman authorities also became aware of the Christians, blaming them for the Great Fire that engulfed the capital (64 CE) and killing their two greatest leaders, Peter and Paul, both of whom died in Rome in the persecutions that followed.

The years following the deaths of the apostles were difficult ones for the church, as it faced not only Roman persecution but also the question of identity: Who are we? And, what is our relation to the Jewish tradition from which we came? How can we know what we are supposed to believe now that the apostles, the ones who knew

Jesus best, are dead? This last question was particularly vexing, especially as certain men and women stepped forward claiming to be in possession of "secret knowledge" (in the Greek, *gnosis*) unavailable to the ordinary believer. These teachings, they claimed, were the only ones capable of providing salvation and had been given by Christ only to the select few.

To combat this movement the church stressed its unique relationship to Christ through the apostles, who had passed on his teachings, complete and unchanged, to those who had succeeded them. In the second century, Irenaeus of Lyons suggested it was for this reason that the true faith could only be found with those *episcopoi*, or "bishops," who could trace their teaching back to the apostles, thus enjoying what became known as "apostolic succession." Therefore, if one wanted to know the correct or "orthodox" faith as opposed to "heresy" (the incorrect faith), one simply had to turn to the bishops who ruled the church in Christ's name. As a result, the bishops became central figures as both leaders of their communities and teachers of the faith, and increasingly it was to them that Christians turned as they faced challenges, both from within the church and from outside it.

Part of the problem was that during this period there were many books and letters, some of which claimed to come from the pens of the apostles, claiming to tell the "real truth" about Jesus's life and teachings. These texts circulated alongside the four Gospels (Matthew, Mark, Luke, and John) for decades before the church began the process of setting the canon ("rule") of Scripture. It decided that only those writings that captured the apostolic tradition and were recognized throughout the church as containing the truth about Christ would be included in what we today call the New Testament, which alongside the Hebrew Scriptures (also called the Old Testament) now constituted the Christians' holy books. The Bible as we know it today was taking shape.

The chief challenge from without remained the Roman Empire, as waves of persecution hit the Christian Church in the decades that followed. The most severe was the persecution overseen by Emperor Decius (250–251 CE), when Christians throughout the empire were required to offer sacrifices to the emperor as a sign of their loyalty. Some did give in (the so-called *lapsi*), but many others refused to do so, oftentimes facing grisly deaths as a result. Yet despite these adversities the faith continued to grow, with churches springing up throughout the empire and taking root in some of the most important cities of the ancient world. In 303 Emperor Diocletian ordered another series of imperial persecutions, but Christianity did more than simply survive this latest attempt to arrest its growth. The church's fortunes were about to change.

According to his biographers, in October 312, in the midst of a civil war among Rome's rulers following Galerius's death, Gaius Flavius Valerius Aurelius Constantinius had a dream. About to go into battle, Constantine saw a sign in the sky containing the Greek letters X and P (the first letters of the Greek word ΧΡΙΣΤΟΣ, or Christ) and heard the words "Under this sign you shall conquer." Constantine knew a heavenly vision when he saw it; he immediately put this mark on all his standards and shields and went off to meet his enemies on the field of battle. His victory the next day at Milvian Bridge was thus attributed to the Christian God, to whom Constantine now felt a particular debt.

Whether or not this account is completely accurate, what happened at the Battle of Milvian Bridge forever changed the fortunes of the Christian Church. The following year Constantine and his co-emperor Licinius issued the Edict of Milan, which granted Christians (and all others) freedom to worship within the empire. Constantine began the process of building churches in Rome and throughout the Holy Land to show his devotion to the faith. His devotion spread to include his family; his mother Helen allegedly found the True Cross (the very cross upon which Jesus died) in Jerusalem while on pilgrimage there. Bishops soon became not only teachers of the faith, but also important political figures, especially the bishops of major cities such as Rome, Alexandria, and Antioch. Within a few short years, Christianity went from being a small persecuted sect to the most powerful religion of the Roman Empire. As Bob Dylan once sang, "You don't need a weatherman to know which way the wind blows," and the wind was clearly blowing Christianity's way.

Becoming a Christian was not necessarily easily: In the early centuries it usually involved a lengthy process of catechesis and training, after which the newly baptized would enter the church at the Easter vigil and be initiated into the mysteries of the faith. Yet during this period Christianity continued to enjoy unprecedented growth—and this brought its own difficulties. With so many embracing the new faith, oftentimes motivated more by political expediency rather than piety, there were those who longed for the days of the martyrs, when Christians proved their dedication to the faith by giving everything, including their lives, for it. Some of these men and women went to the desert, where through ascetic practice they "died to self" and laid the foundations for the monastic movement. Led by men like Anthony the Great, these monks and nuns became an important voice within the church and would come to play an increasingly influential role in the history of Orthodox Christianity.

The other challenge concerned church teaching, as debates arose about the precise nature of Jesus's relation to God: Was he who was lauded in Scripture as "Lord" and "Son of God" a heavenly figure who was a lot like God, or was he God himself? A priest in Alexandria named Arius caused a controversy when he claimed that only God the Father could be eternal, and thus while the Son was the highest of all created beings, he was not, properly speaking, God himself. For many, Arius's thinking made a great deal of sense, because there could only be one God, and by calling Jesus "God," one seemed to introduce a second divinity that would move Christianity away from monotheism and into ditheism.

Constantine, fearing that this debate might destroy the religious unity of the empire, decided to call a council of bishops together at Nicaea in the year 325 in order to settle the matter. At the gathering, now recognized as the first ecumenical (or universal) council of the church, the bishops clarified that the Son was *homoousios* ("the same essence") as the Father, and thus Jesus was indeed God. The argument, later vigorously defended by men like Athanasius "the Great" of Alexandria, was that because only God could save humanity, the savior must himself be God. According to one (perhaps apocryphal) story, debate at the council was so contentious that one of the bishops, Nicholas of Myra, struck Arius across the face and had to be ejected. Nicholas is today celebrated as a model bishop noted for his charitable outreach, becoming the basis for the legend of Santa Claus.

Shortly after the council, Constantine decided to move the capital of the empire, building his "New Rome" on the site of the ancient city of Byzantium. This city, called Constantinople ("Constantine's City"), quickly become the political center of the empire, raising questions about the place of "Old Rome" in the church's governance. For the Constantinopolitans the matter was simple: The religious organization of the church mirrored political realities and since "New Rome" was now the capital, its church should have the same powers and prestige long enjoyed by "Old Rome." The Roman bishops (or "popes") saw things differently. They believed that Jesus had given Peter a unique headship over the church when he gave him "the keys to the kingdom" (Matt. 16:19) and that this role was inherited only by those who succeeded Peter as Bishop of Rome. For the popes the primacy of the Roman church was thus established by Christ himself and could not be changed by the vagaries of politics. Although these two views coexisted relatively peacefully for several centuries, albeit with occasional

1. This icon of the First Council of Nicaea (325) prominently features the Emperor Constantine (middle) and the Nicene–Constantinopolitan Creed. The council was called by Constantine to address the theology of Arius, and it is considered the first ecumenical council of the church.

tension, this fundamental disagreement about the church's structure would eventually have ruinous consequences for the cause of Christian unity.

Constantine had hoped Nicaea would end all debate as to Christ's relationship to God, but in reality it only ushered in a centuries-long process by which the church dealt with the question, "Who is Jesus Christ?" The followers of Arius continued to defend the position of their founder long after his death (which allegedly occurred when God struck him down in 336 by a "violent relaxation of the bowels"). Even those who defended the council's teaching had to confront the questions that logically followed—if Jesus was God, was he also a human being, or simply God wearing a human disguise? If Jesus was God, what about the Holy Spirit? And if the Holy Spirit is divine, how can God be one if God is also three?

Over the next several decades some of Christianity's greatest minds wrestled with these and other questions, producing sermons, tracts, and other theological works in defense of their positions. The fourth-century Cappadocian fathers (Basil "the Great" of Caesarea, Gregory of Nyssa, and Gregory of Nazianzus) were particularly influential in this regard, as they collectively helped shape many of the church's stances regarding Christ, the Holy Spirit, and the Trinity (that is, the belief that God is one essence, but exists as three persons—Father, Son, and Spirit). In 381, just a year after Christianity became the official faith of the Roman Empire, the Council of Constantinople met and affirmed both the divinity of the Holy Spirit and the full humanity of Christ. Jesus Christ was truly God, but he was also fully human, "like us in all things but sin" (Heb. 4:15). The creed that emerged from that council, known today as the Nicene–Constantinopolitan Creed, remains the normative expression of faith for most Christians throughout the world, although small differences among denominations do exist.

Early Christian bishops had other concerns aside from dogma, among the most important being the spiritual health of their congregants. Preachers such as John Chrysostom, Archbishop of Constantinople, often chastised churchgoers for their ostentatious displays of wealth, sometimes in terms modern people might consider harsh. Women such as the Empress Aelia Eudoxia did not much like being compared to harlots for wearing jewelry and makeup, which explains why John was twice exiled during his years as bishop. Yet John's preaching ("Chrysostom" means "golden mouth"), charitable outreach, and devotion to his flock led him to be remembered as a model pastor and saint. Even today, on the Feast of Pascha (Easter), it is the sermon of St. John Chrysostom that is read aloud, inviting all who have come to the table, both the diligent and the latecomer, to feast sumptuously at the banquet Christ has prepared.

Just as Nicaea had not fully answered the questions of Christ's identity, neither had the Council of Constantinople. If Jesus was both true God and true man, did that mean he had two "parts"—human and divine—that remained separate? This position seemed to be implicit in the thought of Nestorius of Constantinople when he denied that the Virgin Mary could be the *Theotokos* ("God-bearer" or "Mother of God"). Mary, he claimed, was the mother of the human Jesus, but since no one could give birth to God, she could not be addressed in prayer as God's mother. A debate ensued, with Cyril of Alexandria arguing against Nestorius that Christ was one and that the divine and human natures united in him in such a way that what could be said about his humanity ("Jesus was born") could also be applied to the divinity ("God was born"). This union of two natures in the one person (or *hypostasis*) of Christ meant that by giving birth to Jesus, who was the second person of the Trinity incarnate, Mary had indeed given birth to God.

Cyril's position was accepted by the Council of Ephesus in 431, but even this did not end the debate. In Alexandria defenders of Cyril's position maintained that the union between God and man in Jesus was such that the two natures merged to create a divine–human "mix." Pope Leo "the Great" of Rome wrote to the Archbishop of Constantinople to oppose this position, setting forth his views in his "Tome to Flavian." When the pope's stance was adopted by the Council of Chalcedon in 451, not everyone was willing to sign on, especially in Egypt, Armenia, and Syria, where many believed that Leo's theology contradicted Cyril's because it continued to speak of "two natures" even after the union. Leo, they maintained, was a Nestorian. For centuries these Christians, commonly known as the Oriental Orthodox, or Copts, continued to recognize only the first three councils, although today scholars on both sides acknowledge that the dispute was more linguistic than substantive.

Chalcedon's embrace of Leo's theology helped validate the pope's growing awareness of his special mission as successor of St. Peter, despite the East's reservations about granting him anything akin to a unique headship over the church. They did continue to honor the pope as first among the bishops, but this did not necessarily entail monarchical rule over the universal church. Instead they looked to the bishops of Rome, Constantinople, Alexandria, Antioch, and Jerusalem as a sort of executive governing board called the "pentarchy" (from the Greek *penta* and *archai*, meaning "five leaders"). The bishops of these cities, called "patriarchs," acted collectively when decisions needed to be taken, but none could claim to wield a power the others did not also have. In fact, even the title "pope" ("father"), now identified almost exclusively with the Bishop of Rome, was (and is) also used for the Patriarch of Alexandria. The Bishop of Rome was first among the bishops, but he was not master over them.

Although the church continued to exist as a single entity, tied in many ways to the boundaries and institutions of the Roman Empire, the growing linguistic and political divide between East and West was beginning to strain the tenuous bonds of unity between them. Increasingly the Latin-speaking world was becoming a stranger to the Greek-speaking East, illustrated by the fact that the greatest of the Western theologians, Augustine of Hippo, was rarely read or translated in the East. When the Western Empire fell in 476 CE, the emerging kingdoms of Europe looked to Rome rather than the emperor to guide them in religious matters. The Emperor Justinian did manage to re-establish some control of Western affairs, imposing his will upon the church and even placing the pope under de facto house arrest for his refusal to attend the Second Council of Constantinople in 553. Yet it was not for this that Justinian is remembered. Rather, today Justinian is best remembered for constructing the church of Hagia Sophia ("Holy Wisdom"), which would become the center of Orthodox life in Constantinople for the next nine hundred years.

Justinian's involvement in church affairs was not novel. Since the time of Constantine the emperor had played a key role in the church's life—calling councils, opposing heresy, even exiling bishops. Some praised the emperor as defender of the faith, seeing his support of the church (and the church's prayers for him) as the manifestation of a God-ordained *symphonia* ("accord") between church and state. Others, like Ambrose of Milan, pointed out the problems of this system, especially when the emperor presumed to wade into doctrinal matters or refused to listen to proper ecclesiastical authorities. Ambrose argued that this kind of caesaropapism (where the state controls and effectively rules the church) must be rejected for "the church belongs to God, [and] therefore ought not to be assigned to Caesar...the Emperor is within the church, not above it."

The seventh century saw the rise of Islam and the first encounters between Christianity and this new faith. Cities that had been Christian centers for centuries, including Jerusalem and Alexandria, now came under Muslim control. It was not until 732 that the advance of Islam was finally halted by Charles Martel and the Franks at the Battle of Tours/Poitiers. Increasingly the Franks became the most powerful kingdom in Europe, aligning themselves with the popes to create a powerful counter to the emperor in Constantinople. By the end of the eighth century the bonds uniting Christendom were still intact, but they were growing ever more strained.

Chapter 2
Byzantines and Franks

The encounter with Islam impacted Christianity in many ways and may have been one of the contributing factors in one of the most acrimonious debates in the Eastern church: the iconoclast controversy. The question was whether the use of icons (pictures of Jesus, Mary, and the saints) violated the biblical commandment prohibiting the worship of graven images (Exod. 20:4–6). Believing that it did, Emperor Leo III and the iconoclasts (the "icon-smashers") began destroying icons throughout the empire, perhaps influenced by Jewish critiques and the Islamic laws against religious images. The defenders of the icons, called iconodules ("venerators of images") or iconophiles ("lovers of images"), argued that Christians did not worship (*latria*) religious images, but instead merely showed them reverence (*proskynesis*) in order to honor the person portrayed. As John of Damascus wrote, "Worship is one thing, veneration another....Full worship we show to God, who alone is by nature worthy of worship...I do not worship matter, I worship the Creator of matter, who became matter for my sake; who willed to take his abode in matter; who worked out my salvation through matter."

In the West, both the pope and the Frankish kings refused to condone the destruction of icons, although Charles "the Great" (better known to history as Charlemagne) feared that the iconodules were advocating a form of idol worship. When, in 787, the Second Council of Nicaea (the Seventh Ecumenical Council) met to sanction the use of icons, the pope immediately gave his approval, but Charlemagne, ever suspicious of the Greeks and their motives, did not. Eventually the two came to terms, and on Christmas Day in the year 800 Charlemagne entered St. Peter's Basilica in Rome, where Pope Leo III anointed him Emperor of Rome. This was significant, for although later historians would refer to the empire centered in Constantinople as the "Byzantine Empire," to its rulers and citizens it was still the Roman Empire and legitimate heir to the Caesars. Now, in an act of unheralded presumption, a barbarian clothed in skins and furs was claiming imperial honors for himself. Worse yet, in order to bolster his political legitimacy, Charlemagne had decided to denigrate the orthodoxy of the Greeks in order to demonstrate why God had transferred rule from Constantinople to his capital at Aachen.

The issue that Charlemagne's court theologians seized upon was the *filioque*. The word itself means "and the Son," and it refers to a line in the Latin version of the Nicene–Constantinopolitan Creed that described the origin of the Holy Spirit. In the original wording of the Creed it said that the Spirit "proceeds from the Father," but in the West, for a variety of theological reasons, it had long been believed that the Holy Spirit also proceeded from the Son. By the seventh and eighth centuries the Creed had been altered in many parts of the Latin-speaking world to affirm this belief—that the Spirit "proceeds from the Father *and the Son*" (in Latin, *filioque*)—and by the time of Charlemagne there were already attacks on the Byzantines for not professing it.

Unfortunately, the Byzantines had problems of their own to deal with, as a second wave of iconoclasm swept the empire in 815. It was not until 843 that the debate finally came to an end with a victory for the iconodules in an event commemorated today as the "Triumph of Orthodoxy." Once again Rome had supported the orthodox position, which caused many in the East, like Theodore the Studite, to praise the pope in glowing terms as "O most divine Head of Heads, Chief Shepherd of the church of Heaven" and "Rock of the faith upon whom the Catholic Church is built." The popes themselves interpreted this acclaim as a recognition of their unique universal authority, which they increasingly tried to exert beyond the traditional boundaries of Rome's jurisdiction. The bishops of the East were in a delicate position, for while they undoubtedly recognized Rome's importance, allowing the pope to interfere in the internal affairs of their churches was something altogether different.

This tension came to a head in the ninth century during the reign of Patriarch Photios of Constantinople, when Pope Nicholas I of Rome refused to acknowledge the legitimacy of his elevation. Although there had been some internal disputes surrounding his selection, and Byzantine politics had played a central role in the appointment, the emperor and clergy of the capital believed it to be an internal matter that did not concern the pope. Nicholas disagreed and declared that Photios should not be recognized. The situation worsened when Photios learned that Frankish missionaries in Bulgaria were introducing their creed—with the *filioque*—into the region, especially as he regarded it as a heretical innovation. By 867 Photios had decided that he had had enough of Nicholas's pretentions and moved to depose him. The so-called Photian Schism had begun.

The death of Emperor Michael III ("the Drunkard"), who had sponsored Photios's appointment, drastically altered the course of events, as the new emperor, Basil the Macedonian, was keen to improve relations with Rome. For this reason in 869 a council (later listed as the eighth ecumenical by Roman Catholics) met in Constantinople to depose Photios, seemingly giving the pope a great victory in his battle against the recalcitrant East. However, in the years that followed, Photios reconciled with his rivals and was restored to the patriarchal throne. In 879–880 another council, this time with the blessing of Nicholas's successor Pope John VIII, officially annulled the decisions taken in 869, recognized Photios as patriarch, and restored peace between Constantinople and Rome. This latter synod, which some Orthodox consider to be ecumenical, ended the so-called Photian Schism, yet neither side had addressed the underlying issues that had helped to bring it about. It many ways the synod merely postponed the division, rather than healing it.

Yet despite these troubles Christianity continued to grow, finally expanding into the Slavic lands thanks to the missionary work of two brothers, Cyril and Methodius. The Bulgarian king Boris I was baptized in 864, with the Byzantine Emperor Michael III as his godfather. Serbia was Christianized soon after, followed by Poland in 966 and Kievan Rus' in 988. According to the *Primary Chronicle*, the story of Christianity in Kievan Rus' began with Prince Vladimir of Kiev, who sent emissaries throughout the world seeking the best religion for his people. When they reached Constantinople they experienced the grandeur of the liturgy in Hagia Sophia, telling Vladimir, "We knew not whether we were in heaven or on earth, such was the beauty of that place." This was enough for the Prince of Kiev, who accepted the Christian faith in its Byzantine form, thus bringing the people of Rus into the church.

For most of the tenth century, East and West experienced vastly different fortunes. The Byzantines were enjoying a cultural, intellectual, and military renaissance under a series of successful emperors, including the aptly named Basil "the Bulgar-Slayer." In Rome things were quite different, as this period is most often described as "the pornocracy" ("the rule of the harlots") or the *saeculum obscurum* ("the dark age"). There was a succession of notoriously unworthy popes, many of whom were either the children or lovers of powerful Roman noblewomen. Often the tool of Roman factions or German kings, these popes were incapable of pressing any claims to authority in the East, where the Byzantines were experiencing their own golden age. The Western church was desperately in need of reform, and by the mid-eleventh century men finally appeared on the scene who could bring it about.

Although often referred to as "the Gregorian Reform" because of its close association with Pope Gregory VII, the reform of the Western church actually began during the reign of one of his predecessors, Pope Leo IX. For Leo and his collaborators, if the church was to be repaired, the pope required authority over anyone, including bishops, kings, and emperors, who might stand in the way of his reforming agenda. Therefore, this period began to see some remarkably strong statements of papal power, although most were aimed not at the Eastern church, but rather at those in the West, like Emperor Henry IV, who dared to challenge the pope's authority. In fact, Leo wanted better relations with the Byzantines for political reasons, which is why in 1054 he sent a delegation led by Cardinal Humbert to Constantinople to negotiate a deal.

The events of July 1054 have come to be regarded as the beginning of the "Great Schism" that divided the Christian world into two halves: the Orthodox East and the Catholic West. But at the time, they appeared to be merely a minor dustup between the cardinal and the Patriarch of Constantinople, Michael Keroularios, both of whom were proud, unbending individuals. After a series of failed meetings Humbert walked into Hagia Sophia and placed a bull of excommunication (a document signaling one's exclusion from the community of the church) against the Patriarch on the altar. This was soon followed by a similar statement against the cardinal from Keroularios. Interestingly, neither document focused on the pope or his powers—instead, Humbert complained that the Byzantine church did not profess the *filioque* and used leavened, rather than unleavened, bread during Communion, while Keroularios protested the Latin practices of forbidding priests to marry and allowing clergy to go beardless.

Within a few years, the quarrel seems to have been largely forgotten by both sides, as each experienced a reversal of fortune. In 1071 the Byzantines suffered one of their most devastating defeats at the Battle of Manzikert, ceding to the Seljuk Turks vast swathes of territory in Asia Minor, which seriously weakened their empire. At the same time the Gregorian Reform was in full swing, thus increasingly placing the pope at the center of Western European affairs. Their positions now reversed from a century earlier, Emperor Alexios I of Constantinople wrote to the pope asking for aid against the Turkish threat, suggesting that a joint campaign against a common enemy might help heal the growing division between East and West. Pope Urban II seized upon the invitation and in 1095 at the Council of Clermont called for an armed pilgrimage to liberate the Holy Land and assist the Byzantines in their hour of need. The Crusades had begun.

The sad irony is that the Crusades, inspired in large part by the desire to bring East and West closer together, actually had the effect of consummating the schism that had grown between them. It was a clear case of familiarity breeding contempt, as the two halves of Christendom had by this time grown so far apart that living in close proximity only emphasized how different they had become. The Byzantines derisively referred to the Latins as "azymites" (those who used unleavened bread) and barbarians, while the Frankish crusaders saw the Greeks as duplicitous heretics who refused to grant the pope his proper role as head of the church. This explains, in large part, why the Western crusaders often replaced Greek bishops with Latins when they took control of cities in the East.

Even the theological methods of the two halves of Christendom were different. In the late eleventh century, Western theology was entering the Scholastic Period (the "age of the schools" in which syllogistic reasoning was emphasized at the newly built universities of Bologna, Paris, and Oxford). Meanwhile, in the East, mystics like Symeon the New Theologian instead emphasized the experience of God through prayer. Granted, the lines were never that sharply drawn; logic and reason still played an important role in the East, just as the scholastic theologians never neglected the role of the experience of prayer, but nevertheless the differences in emphasis were clear.

By the Third Crusade (1189–1192) relations between the Byzantines and the Latins were so strained that many in the West contemplated an attack upon Constantinople in order to put an end to the conflict once and for all. However, it was not until 1203, when an exiled Byzantine prince approached the leaders of the Fourth Crusade, that this actually came to pass. In return for assistance in restoring his deposed father to the throne, Prince Alexios promised the crusaders gold and military aid, along with the pledge that both he and the patriarch would acknowledge the authority of the pope. The crusaders accepted, and soon after arriving in Constantinople, Alexios and his father were once again on the imperial throne. Unfortunately, the young prince had promised far more than he could rightly deliver, and his efforts to come up with the money made him incredibly unpopular among his countrymen. Forced to suspend payments, Alexios now faced the crusaders' wrath.

Urged on by the Latin clergy, who saw this as a perfect opportunity to end the "heresies" of the Greeks, in April 1204 the soldiers of the Fourth Crusade attacked and brutally sacked the city of Constantinople. They looted churches, stole relics, and seated a prostitute on the patriarch's throne in Hagia Sophia, where she sang bawdy songs to the enjoyment of her drunken audience. It was a fatal blow for the cause of Christian unity and one that has not since been forgotten (or forgiven) by many Orthodox. This is perhaps why most scholars today agree that the sack of Constantinople, more so than the events of 1054, marks the real beginning of the schism, since this is the wound that has never truly healed.

For Pope Innocent III, the events of 1204 were a mixed blessing: He was undoubtedly appalled by the crusaders' behavior, but at the same time, with the election of a Venetian patriarch, Constantinople had finally come under his authority. Innocent, who saw this as a chance to finally end the schism on his terms, demanded the obedience of the entire Greek clergy and

2. The sack of Constantinople in 1204 by the armies of the Fourth Crusade remains a bitter memory in the minds of many Orthodox Christians. In 2001, during a trip to Greece, Pope John Paul II apologized again for the actions of the crusaders, imploring God "to heal the wounds of this especially painful memory, which still causes suffering to the spirit of the Greek people."

threatened all those who refused with expulsion from their office. Many did refuse, escaping to the city of Nicaea, where the Byzantines had set up an empire in exile while the Latins ruled in Constantinople. Often there were negotiations between the two sides—the popes offering aid to the Byzantines in exchange for their obedience—but in the end they came to nothing. Despite what the popes wanted to believe, the schism was still very much alive.

Chapter 3
Constantinople and Moscow

In 1261 the Byzantines finally recaptured Constantinople, although by that point the city was only a shell of its former self, most of its treasures having been either brought to the West or sold by the Latins to raise much-needed cash. Emperor Michael VIII, who entered the city to shouts of joy, was the great hero of the hour, but he remained surrounded by enemies and required the pope's assistance if he had any chance of fending them off. For this reason Michael began a series of negotiations with Rome, agreeing that he would recognize the pope's authority in exchange for the military assistance he so desperately needed. Though the emperor was willing to make certain concessions to the pope, most of the Eastern bishops and priests were not, and they told him so in no uncertain terms. Nevertheless convinced that he could eventually command their assent, in 1274 Michael sent representatives to the Second Council of Lyons, where they promised, in the emperor's name, to uphold the Roman faith and give the pope their full obedience.

For many, if not most, of the Byzantines this act constituted a wholesale surrender of the Orthodox faith to the heresies of the Latins. It meant acknowledging the *filioque* as true, the use of unleavened bread in the Eucharist as valid, and the pope as head of the universal church. Supporters of the union were not only guilty of embracing heresy, but also guilty of ethnic betrayal—the charge "You have become a Frank!" was leveled time and again at the unionists in the East. For those who had forgotten their experiences living under Frankish occupation, polemicists stepped forward to remind the Byzantines how terrible the Latins really were, producing lists that detailed the hundreds of ways in which Latin Christianity was deficient or heretical. Despite the best efforts of the emperor and his allies to convince the people that the two churches taught the same faith, the union failed on every level, and by 1285 it was officially rejected by the Orthodox at the Council of Blachernae.

The fourteenth century witnessed an internal debate that rocked the church in the East, as a dispute arose about whether one could, during prayer, have an experience of God as light—an experience similar to what the apostles had had when Jesus was transfigured before them on Mount Tabor. On Mount Athos (the "Holy Mountain"), which had been the home of Eastern monasticism since the ninth century, a group of monks had been practicing a form of prayer called "hesychasm" (from the word "silence"). These hesychasts claimed that by praying the Jesus Prayer ("Lord Jesus Christ, Son of God, have mercy on me, a sinner") in a certain position they could experience the divine light in an unmediated form—a claim that some theologians, like Barlaam of Calabria, felt violated the doctrine of God's unknowability.

The man who came to the defense of the hesychasts was Gregory Palamas, who argued that there was a distinction between the essence of God, which could not be known, and his uncreated energy, which could be known and experienced in hesychast prayer. Not everyone in the East was convinced by Palamas's logic, including a group of allegedly "Latin-minded" theologians who had become admirers of Thomas Aquinas when his works began appearing in Greek translation. Because of their fondness for Aquinas, a misperception has lingered that these opponents of Palamas's theology were never truly "Orthodox," especially as some of them, including Barlaam himself, later joined the Roman church. A series of councils in 1341, 1347, and 1351 later affirmed the legitimacy of Palamas's theology, and today he is celebrated as one of the great saints of the Orthodox Church. The essence–energy distinction is now solidly part of the Orthodox theological tradition, even if questions remain as to whether this entails a real distinction or merely a formal one.

By the fifteenth century the once mighty Byzantine Empire was reduced to the city of Constantinople and a few small territories in Greece. Orthodox Christians had been living under Muslim rule in places such as Syria, Lebanon, and Palestine for centuries, and the recent conquests of Serbia and Bulgaria had placed the Ottoman Turks in control of vast swathes of formerly Christian territory, but Constantinople itself had always withstood the advance of Islam. However, by 1430 the Ottomans had conquered most of the empire's former possessions and were now poised to take its capital. The emperors had little choice but to appeal to the pope, who once again offered the promise of Western aid in exchange for an end to the schism. The difference this time was that Pope Eugene IV offered to convoke a council for the purpose of achieving union, something the Byzantines had been requesting for decades.

In 1438 Emperor John VIII, the Patriarch of Constantinople, and a large delegation of bishops and clergy left Constantinople for Ferrara in Italy, where they hoped to persuade the Latins to drop the *filioque* from the creed and restore peace between the churches. Unfortunately, peace was not so easily achieved, and for the next several months, first at Ferrara and then at Florence, the two sides debated the issues that divided them. The Latins insisted that the *filioque* was true and that the pope had every right to add it to the creed. The Greeks rejected both claims, refusing to believe that the church fathers had ever taught such a thing. The council had hit an impasse, and the weary Byzantine delegates told the emperor that they were ready to quit the council and head home.

It was at this point that the emperor, working with a small group of prominent Byzantine churchmen who were inclined toward union, began to pressure the other delegates. In the end all of them except for Mark of Ephesus signed the union decree, which accepted the *filioque*, the use of unleavened bread, and the pope's headship over the whole church. It was such a complete victory for the Latins that by the time they returned to Constantinople almost all of the delegates had revoked their assent, and Mark became the great champion of Orthodoxy for his refusal to sign. Despite the emperors' best efforts the Florentine union remained unpopular, as the Byzantines generally believed it was "better to die than to Latinize."

While the Constantinopolitans continued to argue the merits of union, the Ottomans prepared for the final assault on the capital. The moment came in 1453, when Sultan Mehmet II brought his forces to the walls of Constantinople, this time bringing not only his army and navy, but also a number of huge cannons capable of blasting the city into submission. On the night of May 28, the last Christian service was celebrated in Hagia Sophia, and on the next day the city fell to Mehmet. Hagia Sophia itself was converted into a mosque, although the Orthodox were granted relative freedom under the leadership of the Patriarch, who became head (or *ethnarch*) of the *Rum Millet* ("Roman nation"). This was an administrative division within the Ottoman Empire that allowed Christians a certain degree of self-governance even if, at the same time, it also guaranteed their status as second-class citizens. The office of patriarch, now granted by the sultan only to those deemed sufficiently reliable, was often sold to the highest bidder, leading at times to a succession of candidates who sought the position solely for personal gain.

In the early sixteenth century Western Europe was rocked by the Protestant Reformation, as Martin Luther and others took issue with Catholic beliefs and practices that they believed to be at odds with Scripture. Some of these reformers thought the Orthodox might be natural allies—after all, the enemy of my enemy is my friend—and wrote to the patriarch for support. However, despite a common rejection of an all-powerful papacy, the Orthodox actually had less in common with the Protestants than with the Catholics, whose teachings on many of the disputed issues were closer to the Eastern view. In an exchange of letters with a group of Protestant scholars from Tübingen, Patriarch Jeremiah II chided them for their refusal to accept church tradition, icons, free will, sacraments, and prayer to the saints. While the Orthodox never truly took sides during the Reformation, many of the catechisms (short books used for teaching the faith) they composed in the years that followed sounded and looked very Catholic.

With so many Orthodox lands under Turkish rule, the center of gravity in the Orthodox world began to shift further east, to Moscow, where a great effort was made to keep the Byzantine legacy alive. Since the disintegration of Kievan Rus' and the invasion of the Mongols in the thirteenth century, the Grand Duchy of Moscow had become a leading power in the region, despite the ongoing threat from the Mongol-ruled Golden Horde. While the Ukrainians and Belarusians found themselves under Lithuanian or Polish rule, the Muscovites under Grand Prince Ivan III were gaining strength, finally ridding themselves of the Golden Horde in 1480 and establishing Muscovy as an independent power. Ivan then married a Byzantine princess and adopted the double-headed eagle (the emblem of the Palaeologus family) on his seal, thus signaling that Moscow had become Byzantium's true successor—the "Third Rome." According to a verse composed by the monk Philotheus of Pskov, "Two Romes have fallen. The third stands. There will not be a fourth."

In the centuries since their conversion, Christians in Ukraine and Russia had developed their own particular way of being Orthodox. Saints such as Sergius of Radonezh, Nil Sorsky, and Joseph of Volotsk helped shape monastic life and spirituality in the region, which flourished in the absence of either Latin or Turkish influence. Having resisted the Florentine union, the Muscovites saw themselves as the preservers of the true faith, increasingly independent of the Constantinopolitan patriarch. When in 1588 Patriarch Jeremiah II was allowed by the sultan to travel north, the Russians invited him to remain in Moscow permanently and exercise his ministry free of Turkish interference. When the patriarch declined the offer they asked for a patriarchate of their own, refusing to let Jeremiah leave until he granted their request. Thus in 1589 Moscow became a patriarchate, technically sixth in the church hierarchy, just behind the five churches of the pentarchy, although Rome's departure from Orthodoxy meant that Moscow was, in reality, fifth.

In parts of Ukraine ruled by the Polish–Lithuanian Commonwealth there were many reform-minded Orthodox who feared Russia's sudden rise to prominence. Yet they were also feeling the pressure to convert to Roman Catholicism, which was the predominant faith of the Polish kingdom. Seemingly stuck between these competing pressures and seeking to reform the Ukrainian church, they approached the pope with a deal: They would acknowledge the union of Florence and the pope's authority, and in return they would be allowed to maintain all their (Orthodox) rites and customs, including a married clergy. The pope agreed, and supported by King Sigismund III, most (but not all) of the Ukrainian bishops subscribed to the Union of Brest (1596), creating what later became known as the Eastern Catholic or "Uniate" church in Ukraine. Considered traitors by the Orthodox and never quite Catholic enough by the Poles, these Eastern Catholics often suffered for their allegiance to Rome, and even today the divisions created by Brest continue to have both religious and political repercussions.

In the decades that followed the Reformation, many Orthodox lands found themselves beset by both Protestant and Catholic missionaries, each hoping to sway the Eastern churches to their way of thinking. This task was made easier by the fact that many Orthodox scholars had moved to the West to study, where they often encountered Western theology for the first time and sometimes became enamored of it. This was very much the case with Cyril Lukaris, a Patriarch of Constantinople whose embrace of certain Protestant ways of thinking led him to compose a statement of faith that sounded very Calvinist, including the idea that God chooses both the elect and the damned, a doctrine known as double predestination. When the Orthodox met to refute these errors at the Councils of Jassy (1642) and Jerusalem (1672) they relied heavily on Roman Catholic teaching, even though the terms and categories they used were essentially foreign to Eastern theology. This is why today some describe the seventeenth through nineteenth centuries as the period of Orthodoxy's "captivity" to Western thought, a period that did not end until the dawn of the twentieth century.

Chapter 4
Persecution and resurrection

The Orthodox Church in Russia suffered two calamities at the end of the seventeenth century. The first occurred in 1652, when Patriarch Nikon of Moscow decided to reform the services of the church and make them conform more closely to what was being done in the Greek-speaking world. He even decided that Russians should change the way they made the sign of the cross—with three fingers (as the Greeks did), rather than two (which had been the Russian custom). Resistance to Nikon's policies, which was widespread, was met with persecution by the state, despite the complaints of many that the reforms had been instituted without adequate consultation. Soon those who continued to oppose the patriarch formed themselves into a movement known today as the Old Believers or Old Ritualists. By the early twenty-first century, the movement had split into two groups—the "priestless" and "priestist"—and although the Russian Orthodox Church has made efforts to reach out to the Old Believers, they continue to reject the reforms of Patriarch Nikon and remain divided from the rest of the Orthodox world.

The second major blow occurred in 1700, when Tsar Peter the Great decided against appointing a successor to the deceased Patriarch Adrian. In fact, he waited twenty-one years before announcing that there would be no successor and that the office of patriarch would be abolished. In his *Spiritual Regulation* (1721),

3. The Transfiguration Church in Kizhi, Russia, with its distinctive wooden structure and twenty-two domes, was built in the early part of the eighteenth century, during the reign of Peter the Great.

which outlined the Russian church's new system of governance, Peter decreed that the church would instead be ruled by a synod of bishops and clergy, with the tsar serving as "Supreme Judge of the Spiritual College." Peter had effectively become bishop of bishops within his empire, enforcing his reforms by defrocking or imprisoning all those who dared defy him.

It is ironic that, as "un-Orthodox" as Peter's move was, given that his system was largely based on the church–state structures found in Protestant countries, in the two centuries that followed the church in Russia enjoyed something of a spiritual renaissance. There was a renewal of theological education, so that by 1808 the number of theological schools and seminaries in Russia had risen to 150, climbing to 340 by 1825. Bishops remained important figures despite the state's increased influence in church affairs.

Philaret of Moscow reformed education and monasticism, publishing the first Russian translation of the Bible in 1858, while Dimitry of Rostov and Theophan the Recluse wrote influential and popular spiritual works. Although some historians have noted the influence of the tsar's Westernizing program on religious art and thought, the era of the *Spiritual Regulation* also produced some of the great saints of the period, the most famous of whom was Seraphim of Sarov, a *starets* (elder) often viewed as the Eastern equivalent of Francis of Assisi. Seraphim greeted those who approached him for spiritual advice with a hearty "Christ is risen!" and despite his physical afflictions (his back was bent after he was left for dead by robbers), he always radiated a sense of resurrection joy. The *starets* became an important part of Russian spirituality, and believers often attributed mystical powers to them, such as the ability to heal or prophesy. Dostoyevsky's novel *The Brothers Karamazov* features the powerful *starets* Father Zosima, and the widespread acceptance of the role of the *starets* perhaps explains why men like Grigori Rasputin could later achieve such influence among the Russian elite.

In the years that followed the Union of Brest, several other local Orthodox churches concluded deals with Rome similar to the one reached by the Ukrainians, creating splits in these communities between those who refused to enter the union and the "Uniates" who did. In Antioch the church divided over the issue in 1729, leading to the creation of the Melkite Greek Catholic Church and the Orthodox Church of Antioch, with the latter largely dependent on the Ecumenical Patriarch in Constantinople. Interestingly, while relations between the Orthodox and their Catholic neighbors were often troubled, in parts of the East (Greece and Cyprus, for instance) there was close cooperation between the two. This ended around the middle of the eighteenth century when both churches began enforcing the ban on sacramental sharing (that is, the practice of allowing members of the other church to receive their sacraments). In fact, in 1755 the Orthodox began insisting that all converts to the faith be re-baptized, the implication being that baptisms performed by other Christian groups were not valid.

On Mount Athos, the spiritual home of Eastern monasticism located on a small peninsula in modern-day Greece, monks such as Nicodemos of the Holy Mountain edited and published some of the great works of Orthodox spirituality. In addition to translating Catholic works that were adapted for an Orthodox readership (for example, *The Spiritual Combat* by Lorenzo Scupoli), Nicodemos was among those who compiled the *Philokalia* ("love of beauty"), a collection of patristic and monastic works that became a centerpiece of Orthodox spirituality. By the beginning of the twentieth century there were more than seven thousand monks living on Athos, including influential Russian saints such as Silouan the Athonite.

With the Ottoman Empire in decline and losing territories throughout Eastern Europe, several areas formerly under Turkish control (Greece, Romania, Bulgaria, and Serbia) sought to have their churches removed from the jurisdiction of the Patriarch of Constantinople. This led to the establishment of local national churches during the nineteenth century, each of them self-governing ("autocephalous") and ruled by either a patriarch or (in the case of Greece) an archbishop. By this time many churches in Syria and the East had also begun to assert their independence, with the church of Antioch choosing an Arab, rather than Greek, patriarch in 1899. While these developments might give the impression that Orthodox churches are supposed to be divided into national or ethnic groups, the fact is that this notion was explicitly rejected in 1872 as a heresy called "ethnophyletism" (from the Greek "nation"). Geography, not ethnic or linguistic concerns, should determine church structures.

Unfortunately, this principle was largely forgotten as Orthodox Christians emigrated to the West, especially to the United States.

As noted in the introduction, Greeks, Russians, Eastern Europeans, and Arabs made their way to America, and each group established its own parishes with links to the mother churches back home. Thus there came to be in the United States "Greek Orthodox" parishes, "Russian Orthodox" parishes, and so forth, oftentimes built within blocks of one another and all having their own bishops and priests, who now found themselves ministering alongside Orthodox clergy of other nationalities. As a result there are currently eight different jurisdictions operating in the United States, many of which believe that the preservation of their national and cultural identity is an integral part of their mission. This situation, which the Orthodox themselves regard as anomalous and even scandalous, means that the structure of the Orthodox Church in the West is remarkably confused, although efforts have been made to begin sorting it out.

Back in Russia, the First World War brought an end to tsarist rule, which allowed the church to re-establish the Patriarchate of Moscow in 1917. Only days earlier the October Revolution had brought Lenin and the Bolsheviks into power, ushering in a time of suffering for the church reminiscent of the third-century persecutions of Decius. Viewing the church as a counter-revolutionary institution, the newly organized Soviet state began closing and destroying churches by the thousands, sending clergy to prison camps or simply killing them outright. When the church tried to resist, as it did when the Bolsheviks ordered the confiscation of icons and vessels used for worship, bishops were executed by firing squad or sent to prison. In all, tens of thousands of bishops, priests, monks, and nuns were killed in the decades that followed. The Russian church survived, but it was now a church of martyrs.

Patriarch Tikhon of Moscow tried to lead the church during that difficult era, but when he spoke out he was placed under house arrest and forced to sign documents recanting his anti-Soviet activity. In 1927 Tikhon's successor, also under Soviet pressure, issued a document demanding the loyalty of all Orthodox Christians to the Soviet state, which many took as a sign that the church had been co-opted by the communists. A group of emigre bishops decided to establish the Russian Orthodox Church Outside Russia (ROCOR), seeing it as a sort of "church in exile" while the communists were in control of the patriarchate. In fact, it was not until 2007, sixteen years after the fall of the Soviet Union, that ROCOR re-established relations with the Patriarchate of Moscow, finally healing the eighty-year breach between them.

If the church in Russia was undergoing persecution, so too was the church in Constantinople. The defeat of Turkey in World War I led to the rise of the secular Ataturk government, which, among other things, reopened Hagia Sophia as a museum after centuries of service as a mosque. However, because of the Greco-Turkish War of 1919–1922 and the resulting Lausanne Convention (1923), all Greek Orthodox Christians in Turkey (except those in Constantinople) were forced into exile. Thousands died in the process, and those that remained in Constantinople were placed under severe restrictions. Riots in 1955 destroyed most of Constantinople's churches and caused many Orthodox to emigrate elsewhere, leaving only a few thousand Christians in a city that was once the thriving center of Eastern Christendom.

The Russian church remained under extreme pressure during the 1920s and 1930s, with the Soviet authorities willing to use any excuse to restrict its freedoms further. This was especially the case during the Terror of 1937–1938, when tens of thousands were persecuted by the NKVD (the People's Commissariat for Internal Affairs) for their faith. The situation briefly improved during World War II, when Stalin needed the cooperation of the church to fight the Germans, but persecution soon returned during the premiership of Nikita Khrushchev. There is no firm count of the number of Orthodox Christians who suffered and died as a result of their faith during the Soviet period, although the number is often estimated to be in the millions. We do know this: Prior to WWI there had been more than fifty thousand churches in Russia, with more than one thousand monasteries and fifty thousand priests. By the late 1980s there were fewer than seven thousand churches remaining, with only twenty-one functioning monasteries. As was the case in Orthodox churches throughout Eastern Europe, the church in Russia was barely clinging to life.

While the Orthodox suffered greatly during this period, the Eastern Catholics in Ukraine suffered just as badly, if not worse. Persecution of their church during Stalin's regime was so relentless that many Eastern Catholics initially saw the invading Germans as liberators. When the war ended Stalin moved to destroy the Eastern Catholics once and for all, orchestrating the pseudo-synod of Lviv in 1946 at which the Ukrainian Catholics were forcibly incorporated back into the Russian Orthodox Church. All Eastern Catholic churches were closed or given to the Orthodox, and bishops and priests who would not comply were killed or imprisoned. On paper the Eastern Catholic Church in Ukraine ceased to exist, and yet it survived underground, awaiting the day when it could emerge from the catacombs.

That day came in 1989, when the Soviet government under Mikhail Gorbachev began easing restrictions on the church, both Orthodox and Eastern Catholic. In Ukraine, Eastern Catholics re-emerged and began laying claim to their former churches, causing the Orthodox hierarchy in Moscow to accuse them of proselytizing (trying to convert members of other churches) and theft. At the same time, the collapse of the Soviet Union in 1991 allowed Orthodoxy to became once again an important part of Russia's political and cultural landscape, with the Patriarch often seen alongside presidents Yeltsin and Putin during important events. The church underwent something of a renaissance, as the number of churches and priests tripled in the decades that followed the USSR's fall. However, tension with Ukraine remained a sore point, for not only were there the Eastern Catholics, but also the breakaway Ukrainian Orthodox churches that demanded independence from Moscow's jurisdiction.

The changes that occurred in Eastern Europe during this period did not mean the era of persecution was over. Arab Christians had been in Syria, Lebanon, and the Holy Land for centuries, surviving and even thriving under the (sometimes hostile) rule of Muslims, crusaders, and Ottoman Turks. Yet rocked both by war and civil strife during the late twentieth century, many of these communities decided the time had come to leave, resulting in a Christian exodus from the Middle East unparalleled in history. This process was exacerbated by the rise of Islamist terrorist organizations, especially ISIS, as the Orthodox increasingly found themselves victims of anti-Christian violence. This is especially true of the Oriental Orthodox (or Copts) in Egypt, where church bombings are a regular occurrence and terrorist acts against Christian communities are all too common.

One of the most interesting aspects of modern Orthodox history has been its re-engagement with the rest of the Christian world. The Orthodox have been a strong presence in the ecumenical movement (the movement to heal the divisions in Christianity) since the beginning, despite occasional calls against associating with "heretics." Relations with the Catholic Church have improved dramatically since the 1960s, when Patriarch Athenagoras of Constantinople and Pope Paul VI first met in Jerusalem after five hundred years of estrangement. Since that time meetings between the pope and the patriarch have become almost commonplace, as has collaboration between Orthodox and Catholic hierarchs and scholars. Although the two sides remain divided over a number of issues, especially the authority of the pope, relations between the two churches are better than they have been in centuries.

In the English-speaking world the Orthodox are still a relatively small group, and yet Orthodox seminaries, theological societies, and intellectual centers have provided them with an influence and visibility far beyond their numbers. The difficulty is that the Orthodox in the United States still remain divided by ethnicity and jurisdiction, making it hard for them to present themselves to the outside world as a single entity. The 1970 establishment of the Orthodox Church of America (OCA) was intended to help the situation by creating an American Orthodox Church, but this only added to the problem when the OCA's self-governing status was rejected by the Ecumenical Patriarch. Still, there is hope—in 2010 the bishops of the United States created the Assembly of Canonical Orthodox Bishops, whose goal is to end the jurisdictional confusion in the United States and bring about something akin to Orthodox unity.

Church unity was the main item on the agenda of the Great and Holy Council of the Orthodox Church held on Crete in 2016, which was intended to be the first meeting of the world's Orthodox bishops in several centuries. Decades in the making, its stated goal was to discuss issues of importance to Orthodoxy and provide a unified witness to the modern world. Unfortunately, the decision of several churches (including the Russian, Bulgarian, Georgian, and Antiochene) to absent themselves meant that most of the world's Orthodox were not represented, and the documents issued by the council remained unacceptable to many. The process of "receiving" (that is, accepting) the council's decisions continues, and yet this should perhaps give the Orthodox themselves some hope. Dialogue, debate, and dispute may occasionally be frustrating, but they also illustrate the vitality of worldwide Orthodoxy as it enters its third millennium.

Chapter 5
Sources of Orthodox thought

Orthodox Christians will often say that theirs is the "church of Tradition," even if defining the exact meaning of "Tradition" (with a capital "T") remains quite difficult for most. But before explaining what it is, it is perhaps necessary to clarify what it is not. First, there is an important difference between "Tradition" and "traditionalism." As the great twentieth-century church historian Jaroslav Pelikan defined them, "traditionalism is the dead faith of the living, while Tradition is the living faith of the dead." In other words, traditionalism is the formal repetition of formulas and ceremonies simply because they are old and established, whereas Tradition maintains a strong sense of continuity with what has come before in order to keep the ancient faith alive and breathing. If Orthodoxy sometimes strays into mere traditionalism—and it occasionally does—it is only because it has forgotten this important distinction.

The other important distinction is between "Tradition" and "traditions." Often and easily confused, traditions are the customs and practices that, over time, have become the ways Orthodox Christians express their faith. These pious customs, like making the sign of the cross with three fingers in order to represent the Trinity, are part of Tradition, yet they are not the same thing. Customs, even long-standing ones, can change or even be dropped depending on circumstances; occasionally they simply fall into disuse or are deemed inappropriate given new developments and contexts. At times the Orthodox themselves have had difficulty distinguishing custom from Tradition (the Old Believer schism is a perfect example of this), but on the whole Orthodoxy knows that some traditions must be preserved while others may not be as essential.

So what, then, is Tradition? For the Orthodox it is the faith as received by the Apostles from Christ, handed down complete without addition or subtraction over two millennia, and lived out in the daily life of the church. Essentially it is the sum total of the church's lived experience—Orthodoxy knows the true faith because for two thousand years it has kept it and lived it. When people came forward with "new" doctrines, the Orthodox knew these teachings to be false because they were not part of the catholic ("universal") Tradition—that is, they did not sync with, as Vincent of Lérins writes in his *Commonitorium*, "what has been believed everywhere, always, by all." This is why in Orthodoxy novelty has always been associated with heresy and why the most damning criticism the Orthodox can make is to call something "new." Liturgy and theology can evolve (and have) over time, but that is fundamentally different from claiming they have ever changed.

Preserving the Tradition, by making sure that it is handed down correctly without adding or subtracting anything, has been one of the distinguishing features of Orthodox Christianity. And while at first Tradition may seem amorphous, the Orthodox believe that over two millennia the Tradition has manifested and expressed itself in a number of concrete ways, allowing the church to know exactly what is contained therein. The most important of these is the Bible, which in Orthodoxy is understood as the infallible Word of God and the centerpiece of the church's Tradition. That said, the Orthodox do not necessarily believe that everything in the Bible (for instance, the accounts of creation in Genesis) must be understood as historical truth, for since the earliest centuries the

43

church fathers have acknowledged that Scripture contains both different literary genres and various layers of meaning.

The relation of the Bible and Tradition in Orthodoxy requires some explanation. During the Reformation in the West, Protestants claimed that God's truth came to us *sola Scriptura* (from the Bible alone), to which the Roman Catholic Church replied at Trent that divine truth is received both from Scripture and from "the unwritten traditions which [were] received by the Apostles from the mouth of Christ himself" (that is, Tradition). To some this implied that Scripture and Tradition were two different sources of God's revelation, as if some truths are received from the Bible and others from Tradition, although to be fair this was not really what the Catholic Church meant to convey.

The Orthodox found both positions inadequate, believing instead that the Bible, as the book of the church, can be understood only if read within the context of the church's Tradition. Thus it was not Scripture *and* Tradition, but Scripture understood *within the context* of Tradition. Scripture is, in a sense, the nucleus around which Tradition itself exists, the most authoritative manifestation of Tradition around which everything else revolves. To take the Bible out of its proper context and interpret it without the Tradition as a guide was to risk misinterpreting it. In the Orthodox view this was exactly what the heretics had done and explains why all theology—from study of the Bible to the study of doctrine—must take place within the context of the church.

Another manifestation of the Tradition is the collection of canons (rules) laid down by the various councils of the early church. These include not only the canons of the seven ecumenical councils (Nicaea [323], Constantinople [381], Ephesus [431], Chalcedon [451], II and III Constantinople [553, 680–681], and II Nicaea [787]), but also those of the various local and regional synods that issued legislation on all aspects of the church's life—morality, relations with non-Christians, when and how to celebrate the liturgy, and so on. Some of these councils were incredibly influential, and many achieved wide acceptance and thus a type of universal or ecumenical status (such as the Council in Trullo [691–692]). The collection of canons most widely used today in the Greek-speaking Orthodox churches is the *Pedalion* (called the "Rudder" because it steers the church), edited by Nicodemos of the Holy Mountain.

Given the emphasis placed in Orthodoxy on adherence to the canons, it could sound like the church is nothing more than a place of laws and rules. However, Orthodox Christianity has always recognized that no matter how important the canons may be, it is ultimately the law of grace that governs Christianity, and thus enforcement of canon law should be characterized primarily by compassion, pastoral sensitivity, and forgiveness. For this reason Orthodoxy recognizes the principle of *economia* ("economy" or "management"), acknowledging that sometimes, because of conditions such as human frailty, church authorities can and should apply or relax the law as needed for the greater spiritual good. *Economia* does not mean that the law can simply be dispensed with or enforced arbitrarily, but it does allow competent authorities (councils, synods, bishops) a certain discretion in order to serve the spiritual needs of the community.

The church fathers, that is, the bishops and teachers of the early church, are another important source of the church's Tradition. Although the "age of the fathers" is sometimes said to close with the death of John of Damascus in 750, the Orthodox also recognize later figures, such as Gregory Palamas, as fathers of the church in the true sense. There are even "church mothers," such as Macrina the Younger, whose devotion to God was chronicled by her brother Gregory of Nyssa, and the Great Martyr Catherine of Alexandria, who refused to renounce her faith even in the face of imminent death. These men and women are celebrated by the Orthodox as privileged witnesses to the true faith and honored for their sanctity of life. Study of the early saints and teachers (called "patristics") is central to Orthodox theology, and oftentimes the correctness of church teaching is judged by its conformity with the *consensus patrum* ("consensus of the fathers"). This is not to imply that the fathers were incapable of theological errors—occasionally even the great saints made mistakes—but the church has long recognized that a minor error in judgment does not detract from a saint's overall greatness or his devotion to Orthodoxy.

For the most part, in the Orthodox Church, there has been a preference for Greek-speaking fathers as opposed to Latin (or Western) figures. There are some important exceptions to this general rule. For example, Cyprian of Carthage's teaching on the unity of the church helped shape later Orthodox thought on the subject, and Pope Leo the Great was fondly remembered in the East for his defense of the true faith at the Council of Chalcedon. Yet for the most part, while Orthodoxy recognizes several early Latin-speaking figures as "fathers," its theological tradition was not greatly influenced by them. This was especially the case with the fifth-century bishop and teacher Augustine of Hippo, among the most influential figures in the Latin Church. In the East Augustine was rarely read, which explains why many of his contributions to Western theology (such as the idea that humanity inherited the guilt of Adam and Eve's "original sin") never permeated the Orthodox consciousness.

Among those who did shape the Eastern tradition and whose icons are found in churches throughout the Orthodox world are saints such as Athanasius of Alexandria, the great defender of Nicene orthodoxy, and John Chrysostom, the fifth-century bishop and preacher who spoke out so bravely on behalf of the poor. Then there are the "Cappadocian fathers": Gregory of Nazianzus, Basil "the Great" of Caesarea, and Gregory of Nyssa, who helped clarify Orthodox teaching on the person of Christ, the divinity of the Holy Spirit, and the nature of the Trinity. In some more conservative Orthodox churches there may also be an icon of the "Pillars of Orthodoxy"—Photios the Great, Gregory Palamas, and

Mark of Ephesus—who are remembered for their work in refuting the heresies of the Latins. And then there are those fathers who came from the non-Greek-speaking East (for example, Ephrem the Syrian), who developed a brand of Christianity unique to itself, preserved today by the churches of Syria, Lebanon, and Iraq.

Naturally, not every Orthodox saint was a great theologian. Mary Magdalene is lauded as "apostle to the apostles" for bearing witness to Christ's resurrection in the face of the apostles' incredulity and doubt. Other fathers and mothers are celebrated not for their erudition, but simply for the holiness of their lives. Mary of Egypt, for example, is remembered for repenting her sinful ways and living the life of a hermit in the desert. There are the "stylites," such as Simeon Stylites, who lived for years at a time atop tall pillars, and "holy fools," such as Andrew the Fool-for-Christ, whose erratic behavior was a witness to the "foolishness of the gospel" (1 Cor. 1:18) preached by Paul. Some saints were "wonder-workers" (such as Gregory Thaumaturgus), others were healers, and many are remembered for bearing witness to the faith through their deaths. These are the martyrs whose blood, according to the Latin theologian Tertullian, became the "seed of the church."

One final source of the Tradition is worship, since it has long been understood that "the rule of prayer is the rule of belief" (*lex orandi lex credendi*). In other words, the church prays what it teaches and teaches what it prays. To understand what the Orthodox believe, simply listen to the liturgy and the prayers of the church, for it is through them that the believer encounters his or her faith. Whereas the Catholic Church has historically been more willing to define its teachings and propose them as doctrines, many teachings of the Orthodox Church have never formally been dogmatized, even though they are recognized liturgically. An example of this is found in the two churches' teachings about the sinlessness of Mary. In 1854 the Catholic Church defined the dogma of Mary's Immaculate Conception—the idea that Mary herself was conceived without the stain of original sin. Orthodoxy does not have this doctrine, which makes sense given that it does not accept Augustine's teaching on original sin, and yet it acclaims Mary as the "all-pure and all-immaculate holy Mother" and "our most holy, pure, blessed, and glorious Lady, the *Theotokos*." Thus each church upholds the belief in Mary's sinlessness—yet one does it dogmatically, while the other proclaims it liturgically.

Chapter 6
"I believe"

The Nicene-Constantinopolitan Creed, which remains the clearest expression of the Orthodox faith, begins with the affirmation "I believe in one God." Belief in one God, or monotheism, is the common element binding together Judaism, Christianity, and Islam despite all their other differences. These three faiths, each in its own way, also share the belief that this one God is incorporeal, outside both time and space, and beyond our comprehension. Thus, despite our desire to speak of God and capture him in language and thought, God himself ultimately remains a mystery. As Gregory of Nyssa wrote centuries ago, "The divine is there where the understanding does not reach . . . it transcends all cognitive thought and representation and cannot be likened to anything which is known." Gregory of Nazianzus went even further: "To tell of God is not possible . . . but to know him is even less than possible."

Yet at the same time Judaism, Christianity, and Islam also affirm that this unknowable God has revealed himself to humanity in a variety of ways—that is, while remaining transcendent, he is simultaneously ever present, making himself known to us as the origin and goal of all humanity. For Christians, God's chief revelation is Christ himself, since he was God in the flesh. There is also the revelation of God in Scripture, where God's word is revealed to us in human language. Orthodox Christians also accept that God has shown himself in the world, where traces of the divine, almost like fingerprints, can be found throughout His creation. These traces allow us to know that God exists, but they do not allow us to know exactly what God is. As Gregory of Nazianzus wrote, "How are you to talk about the being of God? Not by stating what it is but only by rejecting what it is not." God's unknowable essence remains exactly that—unknowable—despite the various ways God is revealed and experienced in this world.

Admittedly, Orthodoxy, like other faiths, has struggled to reconcile these two seemingly contradictory beliefs. It is perhaps ironic that the very men who wrote so eloquently about our inability to know God also wrote dozens of books about him. Yet it was not until the fourteenth century, during the debates about whether God could be experienced through prayer, that Gregory Palamas gave the Orthodox the answer they sought. Palamas did not invent something new, but rather clarified what had long been implicit in Orthodox thought: namely, that there was a distinction between God's unknowable essence and the uncreated energies of God that can be known and experienced in this world. For Palamas the revelations and activities of God in the world are manifestations of God's own energies, and given that they are not something distinct from God, it can truly be said that we experience God himself. At the same time, despite these manifestations in the world, the divine essence remains hidden and ultimately unknowable, defying all description. As John of Damascus had put it centuries earlier, "He has revealed to us what it was expedient to know, whereas that which we were unable to bear he has withheld."

Among the first affirmations Christians make about God in the Creed is that He is the "creator of heaven and earth, of all that is seen and unseen." Leaving aside current debates about evolution and creationism (debates on which the Orthodox Church has not officially taken a position), what Christians profess here is that there is one God, who is both creator and sustainer of the world. There is not a difference, as some early gnostic sects wanted to claim, between the God who created the material world and the spiritual God who lies beyond it. The material world is not inherently evil, nor are we trapped on this earth as punishment for some sort of primordial sin. Instead, what the book of Genesis tells us is that creation is a deliberate and gracious act of a loving God and that creation itself is good because God himself made it that way. According to John of Damascus, "Because the good and transcendentally good God was not content to contemplate himself, but . . . saw fit that there should be some things to benefit by and participate in his goodness, he brings all things from nothing into being and creates them, both visible and invisible."

Everything noted here thus far about God—that he is one, unknowable creator—can equally apply to the theology of Islam and Judaism. Christianity is distinct from the other Abrahamic faiths, however, in the belief that the one God exists as a Trinity of persons—that God is Father, Son, and Holy Spirit. In fact, one of the first things one might notice when attending Orthodox worship is how little "God" is actually mentioned. Instead, Eastern Christian liturgy consistently speaks about "Father, Son, and Holy Spirit, the Trinity one in essence and undivided." Rarely are prayers addressed to "God" as they are in Western Christianity. God is one, but at the same time he is three, and this trinitarian/personalist emphasis is one of the hallmarks of Orthodox thought.

Conveying the belief that God was concurrently one and three was not easy for the early church. On one side there was a temptation toward "tritheism" (the belief that there were three gods who simply worked closely together), and on the other side there was a movement toward "modalism" (the idea that God was one and simply filled three different roles throughout salvation history—as creator, redeemer, and sanctifier). Between this Scylla and Charybdis stands the Christian belief that there is one divine essence (in Greek, *ousia*) shared by the Father with the Son and the Holy Spirit, and thus all three persons of the Trinity are fully divine, coequal, and coeternal.

Another problem for the early church was figuring out how the three persons in God related to one another, for there was a temptation to think that the Father alone was "God," while the Son and Holy Spirit were somehow lesser entities. It is true that Orthodoxy affirms the Father to be the source and origin of the divinity, "the unique essential begetter of the unique *Logos*, [the Word]...and the fount of the unique everlasting life, the Holy Spirit," in the words of Maximos the Confessor. Yet at the same time, Orthodox Christians believe that while the Father is the sole cause or origin of the Trinity, this does not imply any temporal priority or an inequality of nature. There was never a time when the Son and the Spirit were not with the Father and with him fully sharers of the divine nature. According to Orthodox belief the three persons exist in an eternal state of *perichoresis*, understood as a mutual indwelling of the persons without any sort of confusion between those "qualities" that make each person who he is. All three persons are God, but only the Father is the cause within the Trinity, only the Son is begotten, and only the Spirit proceeds (or comes forth) from the Father.

This last affirmation, that the Holy Spirit proceeds from the Father, leads to the issue that still today divides the Orthodox from Western Christians: the *filioque*. The word itself means "and the Son," and it refers to the Latin belief that the Spirit proceeds not only from the Father, but also from the Son. When the Franks added this word to the Creed in the ninth century, the Orthodox objected, believing that the Father alone was cause within the Trinity, and thus the Father alone must be responsible for the Spirit's coming-to-be. To assert, as the Latins seemed to, that the Son was another cause of the Spirit's existence would be to confuse the qualities that make each person in God distinct. Although subsequent Protestant and Catholic theology has tried to allay Orthodox fears around the subject, the Orthodox continue to believe that attributing any degree of causality to the Son is impossible, which is why the continued presence of the *filioque* in the creeds of the Western churches remains so problematic for them.

To declare that each person in God has distinct qualities is not to imply that the three can somehow be separated. All three persons are active in creation, as God creates through his Wisdom (the Spirit) and his Word (the Son), as Irenaeus of Lyons explained centuries ago. All three persons are active in salvation history, because it is the Father who sends the Son into the world, who in turn is made flesh by the power of the Holy Spirit. It is this same Holy Spirit, given to humanity by the resurrected Jesus, who allows us to cry out, "Jesus Christ is Lord, to the glory of God the Father" (Phil. 2:11).

For many of the church fathers, the Trinity was revealed not only in salvation history, but also in the trinitarian makeup of the human person, composed as we are of body, soul, and spirit. This was not an accident, since all Orthodox thinking about the human person begins with the biblical truth that humanity was made "in the image and likeness" of God (Gen. 1:26) and thus somehow stands as an icon of the divine. Given that all people are icons of God, carrying within them the *imago dei* ("image of God"), each person is capable of discovering God both within himself or herself ("The Kingdom of God is within you," Luke 17:21) and within others. This recognition that God dwells in all people demands that we treat everyone with the greatest respect, for as Clement of Alexandria wrote at the beginning of the third century, "Having seen thy brother, thou hast seen thy God."

Because humanity is made in God's image, the Orthodox hold that individuals are created by God not only to be with him, but also to be like him, by using their God-given free will to grow in his likeness. This concept of *theosis* (or deification)—the belief that humanity's destiny is to become more like God—stands at the center of Orthodox thinking about the human person and his or her destiny. The very purpose of humanity, the very reason for which it was created, is to use its freedom in such a way that humans become "fellow-workers with God" (1 Cor. 3:9) and thus more like God through the indwelling of His spirit. This *synergeia* (synergy) between free will and divine grace, the harmony and unity between God and humanity, is what God intended for his creation. But then something happened.

According to Genesis, Adam and Eve rejected the proper use of their free will; instead of choosing to be with God in loving obedience, they surrendered to the serpent's offer to "be like God" (Gen. 3:5) in a manner of their own choosing. In their disobedience they ruptured their communion with God and lost their likeness to him, even though they still retained within them the divine image, albeit now scarred by sin. Although the Orthodox do not adhere to a belief in inherited guilt for Adam's sin like Western Christians (the concept of "original sin"), they do maintain that the unity of humanity is such that what happened to Adam and Eve somehow affects us all. As a result of this first sin all humanity became subject to sickness and death, consumed by a self-love that separates us both from God and from one another.

Had things ended there, humanity's fate would have been bleak indeed, but the "good news" of the Christian gospel is that despite its disobedience, God decided not to abandon humanity to sin and death. Instead, the Father sent the Son into the world where, according to the Creed, "for us men, and for our salvation, he came down from heaven, was made flesh by the Holy Spirit and the Virgin Mary, and became man." Because he was the same substance (*homoousios*) as the Father and thus a perfect likeness to Him, Jesus became the "new Adam" who could once again manifest the perfect image and likeness of God. Even more importantly, Christ gave the world the Holy Spirit so that, through the indwelling of his spirit, believers could die to self and become more like Christ and thus more like God. Deification or *theosis*, our transfigured or graced communion with God and the very reason why humanity was created, was once again possible. God had reached down and touched a sinful humanity and, in doing so, raised it up unto Himself. As Athanasius of Alexandria said centuries ago, "God became incarnate that we might be made God."

Of course, the old enemies remained to be overcome: namely, sin and death. The Orthodox belief, proclaimed with great joy all throughout the Paschal (Easter) liturgy, is that after obediently accepting death on the cross Christ was raised by God from the dead, "trampling down death by death, and upon those in the tombs bestowing life." No longer would death be the end, because with Christ's resurrection came the promise that all who believed in him would similarly be raised to new life. Yes, people would still fall ill and eventually die—this was simply part of the human condition—but now believers could do so without despair, because Christ's resurrection was a foretaste of what was to come.

4. In the icon of the Resurrection, Christ raises Adam and Eve from their tombs, symbolically bringing all of humanity to new life. Orthodox Christians celebrate the resurrection of Christ as the great victory over sin and death.

For those familiar with Western Christianity, especially evangelical Protestantism, this description of humanity's salvation in Christ may seem incomplete. While the West has usually emphasized the salvific death of Christ as payment for sin, using words like "atonement" or "satisfaction," the East has instead stressed the importance of the resurrection in bringing humanity to new life. It is not that the West forgets Easter Sunday or that the East forgets Good Friday, but rather a matter of emphasis. For the Orthodox, when Christ willingly accepts the cross and "he who hung the Earth upon the waters is hung on the tree" (Fifteenth Antiphon of Good Friday), death itself is transformed and the terrifying moment of humanity's end is turned into a victory.

Even with Christ's victory over death, sin remained part of the human condition and had to be overcome via the power of God's grace. The issue, as ever, was free will, which instead of working synergistically with God remained distorted by the sinful self-love that separated humanity from Him in the first place. This perversion of the will predisposes people to choose perceived goods (sensual pleasure, avoidance of pain) instead of their ultimate end, which is why humanity finds it so difficult to obey God. Even Jesus, who was God and whose human will was in perfect conformity with that of the Father, was tempted to disobey (as in the Garden of Gethsemane on the night before his death), but never did. Thus what is required of Christians is essentially a retraining or reorientation of the will so that through asceticism (self-discipline), believers can conform their wills to Christ's and thus, like him, always choose what God wants rather than what they personally desire. In the words of Maximus the Confessor, in this process of dying to self another incarnation takes place in the believer whereby Christ's presence "grows fat by the practice of the virtues" and God's likeness is once again restored. The Christian dies to sin to the extent that Christ lives within them.

Why God became man

Orthodox theology rarely talks about salvation in terms of "satisfaction" or "justification," preferring instead to concentrate on the transformative power of the Holy Spirit as we are made more like Christ in love. According to the Liber Asceticus *of Maximos the Confessor, the great seventh-century saint and theologian, this transformation was the very purpose of the incarnation.*

Our Lord Jesus Christ, being God by nature and, because of His kindness, deigning also to become man, was born of a woman and made under the law as the divine Apostle says, that by observing the commandment [of love] he might overturn the ancient curse on Adam.... Instead of hate he set forth love, by goodness he cast out the father of evil.... He showed us a godlike way of life; he gave us holy Commandments and promised the Kingdom of Heaven to those who lived according to them.... From the condemnation of ancestral sin he absolved [us] by obedience; by death he destroyed the power of death so that as in Adam all die so in him all shall be made alive.... He sent the Holy Spirit as a pledge of life, and as a help to those who struggled to keep his Commandments for their salvation. This, in brief, is the purpose of the Lord's becoming man.—Maximos the Confessor

None of this would be possible without God's help; therefore, the Orthodox wholeheartedly affirm the absolute priority of God's grace over the will in the process of salvation. Christians are "fellow-workers" with God (1 Cor. 3:9), and there is a synergy between free will and grace, but it is far from an equal partnership. Believers cannot save themselves, yet neither can they be saved alone. In fact, called to live in communion with one another and to recognize Christ in all people, Christians are called to demonstrate the same *philanthropia* (love of humanity) that the Father showed humanity in the gift of his Son. For this reason Orthodox Christians have long been advocates of what the modern world calls "social justice," manifesting their love of Christ in acts of loving service to "the least of [his] brothers and sisters" (Matt. 25:40). From the Orthodox perspective, attending Sunday liturgy is all well and good, but as John Chrysostom is alleged to have said, "if you cannot recognize Christ in the beggar at the church door know that you will not find him in the chalice."

Chapter 7
"Pray unceasingly"

Orthodox spirituality begins with the presupposition that humanity was created to be in communion with God and that this state is not only achieved after death, but also attainable in this life. At the same time, Orthodoxy recognizes that because of humanity's fallen nature, this goal is not easily obtained. Too often distracted and preoccupied with worldly matters, humanity finds union with God difficult, if not impossible, to achieve. Yet Orthodoxy teaches that with the help of God's grace believers can, and indeed must, move closer to God in communion and strive to do God's will in all things. This, in short, is the goal of the spiritual life, and it occurs, according to Maximos the Confessor, when the Christian comes "to possess these three virtues: love, self-mastery, and prayer. Love tames anger; self-mastery quenches concupiscence; prayer withdraws the mind from all thoughts and presents it, stripped, to God himself."

Love has always been considered the chief Christian virtue. St. Paul writes, "If I have all faith, so as to remove mountains, but do not have love, I am nothing.... Faith, hope, and love abide, these three; and the greatest of these is love" (1 Cor. 13:2, 13). Christ himself taught that the greatest commandment is to "love the Lord your God with all your heart, and with all your soul, and with all your strength, and with all your mind; and your neighbor as yourself" (Luke 10:27). The great saints have also emphasized this link between love of God and neighbor; John Chrysostom in particular teaches that our treatment of the poor is the best indication of our love for Christ. "Would you honor Christ's body?" he asked his congregation. "Then do not neglect him when naked; do not honor him here [in church]...while neglecting him perishing outside of cold." It is for this reason that Orthodox Christianity has long been associated with the idea of philanthropy (from the Greek *philanthropia*, or "love of humanity") and with the necessity of charitable outreach toward those in need. There were hospitals for the sick and charities for the homeless in Constantinople centuries before "social justice" became a part of the modern vocabulary.

The importance of self-mastery or asceticism in the process of drawing closer to God has long been noted by Orthodox spiritual writers, although its purpose has frequently been misunderstood. In Orthodoxy the goal of detachment and fasting is not to rid oneself of material things because the world is inherently evil. On the contrary, asceticism is necessary because it allows us to see God in all creation, unburdened by the human passions and excessive self-love that too often focus our attention on how the world can serve our immediate needs. This is why the Orthodox place such a premium on asceticism; they hold that only through proper use of the world can believers come to discern more closely God's presence in it. Fasting days and seasons (of which the Orthodox calendar contains many) essentially become opportunities not only to refocus the Christian's attention on what really matters, but also to draw closer to the reality of God's indwelling in all things. Fasting is thus not an end in itself, but rather the means of opening oneself to receive something greater. This dynamic of self-emptying only to make room for God is most clearly seen in the Lenten Prayer of St. Ephrem the Syrian, in which Orthodox Christians ask the Lord to take from them "the spirit of sloth, despair, lust of power, and idle talk" and to give them instead "the spirit of chastity, humility, patience, and love." In this way believers put away "the old self, corrupt and deluded" and clothe themselves anew, "according to the likeness of God in true righteousness and holiness" (Eph. 4:22–24).

Prayer is at the very center of Orthodox life, whether it is public (for example, the Divine Liturgy) or private. For the Orthodox prayer is not merely a matter of establishing a dialogue with God, but rather a means of experiencing God. This requires not only a great deal of effort on our part (since we are prone to weakness and spiritual "cooling"), but also a gift from God, who makes such prayer possible. For centuries Orthodox spiritual writers have stressed the importance of setting aside specific times for prayer, both for the recitation of the psalms (*orthros*, *vespers*, and *compline*, for example) and for personal offerings of thanksgiving and supplication. Recognizing that the spiritual journey is a difficult one, beginners are often encouraged to seek out an *abba* or *starets* (a spiritual father) who can guide the believer along his or her way. Because these individuals are usually priests they can also serve as confessors, which is beneficial given that frequent confession has long been regarded as a great help in the spiritual journey.

St. Paul's injunction to "pray without ceasing" (1 Thess. 5:17) lies at the heart of the nineteenth-century Russian spiritual classic *The Way of the Pilgrim*. In the book the main character, who is never named, reads this passage and goes on a pilgrimage to discover how he can accomplish this seemingly impossible feat. Along the way he is taught the Jesus Prayer ("Lord Jesus Christ, Son of God, have mercy on me, a sinner"), which he is told to pray hundreds of times of day. With his prayer rope (called a *chotki* in Russian or *komboskini* in Greek) in tow, the protagonist travels all over Russia and learns from his encounters with others how best to achieve union with God in prayer.

There are other spiritual works that have helped shape the Orthodox tradition, including *The Ladder of Divine Ascent* by John Climacus, which describes the soul's ascent to God and the many perils it may encounter along the way. *The Commentary on the Divine Liturgy* by Nicholas Cabasilas not only explains the church's liturgy but also explains the mystical meaning of each action. Another Orthodox spiritual classic, *The Unseen Warfare*, has an interesting history, as it was originally composed by the Roman Catholic author Lorenzo Scupoli following the Protestant Reformation. Scupoli's work, titled *Il combattimento spirituale* (*The Spiritual Combat*), eventually found its way to Mount Athos, where Nicodemos of the Holy Mountain adapted it for Orthodox use. It was further altered by Theophan the Recluse, and in the early twentieth century it became an important part of the Russian spiritual tradition. Nicodemos of the Holy Mountain was also among those responsible for editing the *Philokalia*, a collection of patristic and monastic texts on prayer that sits at the center of Orthodox spiritual life.

The fact that most of the texts were written or edited by monks testifies to the important role monasticism has played in shaping the Orthodox spiritual tradition since the early centuries of the church. By the time the "Father of Eastern Monasticism," Anthony the Great, began his life in the Egyptian desert in the fourth century, there were already men and women living solitary lives there in search of God. Later some of these monks formed themselves into cenobitic communities (from the Greek for "common life"), where they came together for prayer and meals guided by a spiritual *abba*, or "father." In time these communities formed rules to govern themselves, the most common in the East being the Rule of St. Basil. According to the *Sayings of the Desert Fathers*, the monk's life work consisted of "obedience, meditation, not judging others … not taking but rather giving to others, not being proud in his heart, nor maligning others with his thoughts, not filling his stomach, but in all things behaving with discretion."

Throughout Orthodox history monasticism has played a key role in many of the theological debates that have shaped the faith. During the eighth and ninth centuries, when there were as many as one hundred thousand monks in Byzantium, monastic opposition to the emperors' campaigns against the icons was key to the iconoclasts' ultimate defeat. In the thirteenth and fifteenth centuries, during negotiations over union with the Catholic Church, the monks were a pivotal factor in ensuring the failure of both the union of Lyons and the union of Ferrara-Florence. During the hesychast debate of the fourteenth century it was Gregory Palamas's defense of the Athonite monks that led him to uphold the belief that one could experience God directly in prayer.

Mount Athos, more commonly referred to as the "Holy Mountain," is a community of twenty self-governing monasteries located on a small (350 square kilometers) peninsula in modern-day Greece. Athonite monks come from all over the Orthodox world, as do pilgrims seeking spiritual advice and comfort. According to the tradition, it has been the center of Orthodox monasticism since the Virgin Mary landed there during a voyage to Cyprus—the only woman ever permitted to set foot on the Holy Mountain. Even in the early twenty-first century, the monks of Athos continue their centuries-long practice of forbidding females (both human and animal) from visiting, despite occasional pressure from the European Union to end this policy. Yet life on Mount Athos remains very much as it did centuries ago, aside from the occasional concession to the modern world: Today the Holy Mountain has its own website and even offers virtual tours of some of the monasteries.

The ninth-century victory over iconoclasm, secured with monastic assistance, ensured that icons (that is, images of Christ, Mary, and the saints) remained one of Orthodoxy's most distinguishing features. Unlike religious imagery in the West, which often had an aesthetic or pedagogical function (namely, instructing the illiterate in the faith), icons in the East traditionally served a different purpose. Sometimes called "windows into heaven," icons draw the believer closer to the person or event depicted, allowing him or her to see in the icon something more than a mere image. Most depict Christ, for it is through him, who is God incarnate and the "image of the invisible God" (Col. 1:15), that we have this unique point of contact with the divine. At the same time, images of God the Father are quite rare in the Orthodox tradition, although they do exist.

In Orthodox spirituality icons are often used in prayer, and it is common for believers to light candles in front of them and kiss them when they enter or exit the church. Although this might look like "idol worship" to the outsider, since the eighth century the church has been clear that there is an important difference between worship (*latria*) and reverence (*proskynesis*), God alone being worthy of the former. The reverence given to icons merely demonstrates the honor due to the one portrayed and does not in any way imply that the icon itself is being worshipped.

In Orthodox tradition, icons are usually described as having been "written" rather than painted, and it is rare that one finds the artist's name on the icon itself. Although there have been famous iconographers—the fifteenth-century Russian iconographer Andrei Rublev prominent among them—one does not usually speak about their "style" the way one might when discussing artists such as Michelangelo or Leonardo da Vinci. In fact, icons are not understood as individual statements, but rather as ecclesial ones, which is why they typically stick to prescribed types; that is, Christ and Mary generally look the same in most icons regardless of when or where they were written. That said, one can usually tell a Greek or Russian icon apart from its Egyptian or Syrian counterpart. This is especially true of Russian icons written during the eighteenth and nineteenth centuries following the reign of Peter the Great, when iconographers adopted a more Western style of painting, but this is the exception rather than the rule.

Another distinguishing feature of Orthodox spirituality is the strong emphasis placed on Mary, who is almost exclusively addressed as the *Theotokos* ("God-bearer" or "Mother of God") in

5. A sixth- or early seventh-century icon of the *Theotokos* and Child between Saints Theodore and George. Reverence for the mother of Christ is an important part of Orthodox spirituality, because her "yes" to God allows for the incarnation.

the church's prayers and devotions. There are several feasts in the Orthodox calendar that celebrate events in Mary's life (for example, her birth, presentation in the Temple, and "falling asleep"), and in most churches her icons are displayed prominently. Frequently the image of Mary as *Panagia* ("all-holy") appears on a church's apse (the domed wall above the altar), and among the most common icons in Orthodoxy is the *Deesis*—an image of Christ with Mary and John the Forerunner (John the Baptist) standing on either side. In the Divine Liturgy Mary is called "ever-blessed, and all-blameless ... more honorable than the Cherubim, and more glorious beyond compare than the Seraphim," and in one prayer in particular believers cry, "Most Holy *Theotokos* save us!"

Roman Catholics, who share a similar devotion to Mary, have few problems with the "exalted Mariology" of the Orthodox. For them, as for Orthodox Christians, Mary's "yes" to the incarnation makes salvation in Christ possible, earning her a unique place among the saints as the one who stands closest to her son. Yet Protestant Christians have historically been uncomfortable with prayers to Mary and the saints, believing as they do that it detracts from the centrality of Jesus Christ as "the one mediator between God and man" (1 Tim. 2:5).

To the Orthodox mind, veneration of Mary and the saints does not detract from the person of Christ, but rather magnifies him who "is glorified in his saints" (1 Thess. 2:10). The saints, joined to present-day believers by bonds of faith and love, remain active parts of the church and continue to intercede on its behalf before Christ in heaven. Their icons and relics (a saint's earthly remains or pieces of an important religious object) remind Christians of the saints' heroic virtues and encourage them to emulate the saints in the holiness of their lives. Churches often have small relics of important local saints that can be displayed for veneration

The Akathist Hymn to the *Theotokos*

Traditionally (if not accurately) ascribed to the sixth-century Byzantine hymnographer Romanos the Melodist, the Akathist Hymn contains twenty-four sections that salute the Virgin Mary and her singular role in salvation history.

An Angel of the first rank was sent from heaven to say to the *Theotokos*: Rejoice! And perceiving You, O Lord, taking bodily form, he stood in awe and with his bodiless voice cried aloud to her as follows:

Rejoice, through whom joy shall shine forth;
Rejoice, through whom the curse shall vanish.
Rejoice, fallen Adam's restoration;
Rejoice, redemption of Eve's tears.
Rejoice, height that is too difficult for human thought to ascend;
Rejoice, depth that is too strenuous for Angels' eyes to perceive
Rejoice, for you are the throne of the King;
Rejoice, for you hold him Who sustains everything.
Rejoice, star that shows forth the Sun;
Rejoice, womb in which God became incarnate.
Rejoice, through whom creation is renewed;
Rejoice, through whom the Creator becomes an infant.
Rejoice, O Bride unwedded.

during certain feasts. In the United States this includes such figures as Saints Raphael of Brooklyn and Alexei Toth of Wilkes-Barre, both of whom contributed to the growth of Orthodoxy in the United States in the nineteenth century. Yet not every saint was a bishop—the Orthodox also celebrate married men and women (for example, Joachim and Anna, the parents of Mary) and modern-day saints such as Elizabeth Feodorovna, the German princess (and later nun) who was murdered by the Bolsheviks in 1918 and canonized alongside hundreds of "new martyrs" in Russia. Saints, like Christians themselves, come in many different shapes and sizes.

Chapter 8
"One, holy, catholic, and apostolic Church"

Since its beginning, Christianity has affirmed that believing in Christ necessarily means belonging to a community of believers. As written in the Acts of the Apostles, "All who believed were together and had all things in common.... Day by day, as they spent much time together in the temple, they broke bread at home and ate their food with glad and generous hearts" (Acts 2:44–46). One could never be a Christian alone, for being a believer necessarily connected one, by virtue of a common baptism, with all those who had accepted the gospel.

When the Bible speaks of the community of believers it uses several images, including that of a bride and that of the body of Christ. This is important, because all too often the church is viewed solely as an institutional or hierarchal reality, without reference to its essentially theological nature. For the Orthodox the church is the assembly (in Hebrew, *qahǎlā'*, or in Greek, *ekklesia*) gathered together by Christ himself in order to be his ongoing presence in the world. In the church believers become "the People of God," called to be "a royal priesthood" and servants to both God and the world. Like Christ, the church is both a divine and a human reality, never fully reducible to the earthly institutions and structures that surround it. The church is more than a building or a bishop; it is a mystery.

Because membership in the church is considered essential, the church fathers are clear that exclusion from the community, either by expulsion or by choice, put one's eternal salvation in jeopardy. According to Cyprian of Carthage, "He cannot have God as his father who does not have the church as his mother." Elsewhere Cyprian put this even more starkly, writing, "Outside the church there is no salvation" (*extra ecclesiam nulla salus*), the logic being that the church is the sole source of the saving grace offered by Christ. The phrase *anathema sit* ("Let him be banned"), a judgment passed on those who subscribed to some deviant practice or belief, thus became the most severe punishment the church had to offer. The sentenced party would be considered "excommunicate" ("out of communion" with the church), effectively breaking the bonds joining him or her to the saving community of Jesus Christ.

Among the central beliefs of the Orthodox Church is that Jesus, during his earthly ministry, gathered about him a core group of followers to whom he entrusted both his teachings and the continuation of his ministry. These apostles (from the Greek word *apostolos*, meaning "one who is sent out") bore the task of not only spreading the good news throughout the world, but also of maintaining its purity when challenged by false teachings. These apostles were led by Simon Peter, who, as *coryphaeus* or "choirmaster," had a recognized role as spokesman for the group both before and after the resurrection of Jesus. Yet despite his unique position, Orthodox theology has always emphasized Peter's place among the apostles, rather than his authority over them, and unlike Roman Catholic teaching, the Orthodox Church has never viewed Peter as having any unique powers not also given to all. The apostles as a group were given "the keys of the kingdom of heaven" (Matt. 16:19), the power to forgive sins, and the authority to govern the church following Christ's return to the Father.

To help them in this task, Christ sent the Spirit, or *paraclete* ("advocate"), upon the apostles on the day of Pentecost, which is why the church could properly be called the dwelling place of the Holy Spirit. Thus empowered for their ministry, the apostles began the task of preaching the gospel throughout the world, always faithful to the truth they had received from Jesus during his earthly life. When unacceptable teachings arose—and they arose quite early on—it was the apostles' task to correct them and to ensure the true faith. For example, a debate arose over whether Greek converts to Christianity needed to accept the Jewish law; Paul argued that they did not, while James and others maintained that they should. At that time, "the apostles and elders met to consider this question" (Acts 15:6). At this gathering, usually referred to as the Council of Jerusalem (ca. 50), the group decided in favor of Paul, and Christianity was forever changed. This model of collective leadership and decision-taking became for the Orthodox the norm and helps explains the importance in Orthodoxy of the synodal principle.

Synodality, alternately called conciliarity or *sobornorst*, is the idea that the mind of the church is best expressed when it comes together in a synod or council, and the voice of the Holy Spirit is made known through the consensus of those gathered. The Council of Jerusalem is in many ways the model for the concept, but the Seven Ecumenical Councils—the gatherings of bishops between 325 and 787 that met to decide matters of doctrine and discipline—stand as the prime examples of how the synodal principle works within Orthodoxy. There have been many local or regional synods since that time, but it was at these seven gatherings that the faith of the church was set, and the voice of the Holy Spirit was heard in the chorus of the assembled bishops.

The bishops (in Greek, *episcopoi*), as the successors of the apostles, inherit both the authority and the responsibilities given to that first group of Jesus's followers. Assuming the office in a direct line from the apostles themselves, these bishops enjoy "apostolic succession" and are the true interpreters of the faith and the guarantors of orthodox teaching. They bear the responsibility for governing the universal or "catholic" church, which they do first and foremost by leading a local community of believers (called a diocese) as their spiritual father. As leader of the local church, the bishop makes Christ present to the community and in the Eucharist manifests the universal church with whom he is one, via the bond of communion.

Although Orthodoxy emphasizes the essential equality of all the bishops, at the same time it has recognized that certain bishops, for a variety of historical reasons, have achieved a standing beyond the boundaries of their diocese. Metropolitan bishops, for example, governed the important cities of the empire and were responsible for coordinating action among the smaller dioceses of the nearby region. Early on, five cities were recognized as having a kind of super-metropolitan status because of their political importance or because they had been founded by the apostles. These patriarchates of Rome, Constantinople, Alexandria, Antioch, and Jerusalem collectively became known as the pentarchy (from the Greek *penta* and *archai*, meaning "five leaders"); they were given a special role in coordinating the activities of the church. In Orthodox thought they were often compared to the five fingers of the hand or the strings of a lyre, always acting in harmony and no one more important than the others—even if there was an acknowledged *taxis* ("order") to them that placed Rome first.

This matter of Rome's primacy or "first-ness" became (and still is) one of the chief causes of the schism between Orthodoxy and Roman Catholicism. In Roman Catholic theology Rome's primacy is based on its foundation by Peter and Paul, specifically on the pope's succession from Peter as prince and chief of the apostles. Just as Peter was leader of the Twelve and entrusted with the keys of the kingdom, so too the pope has a singular role as head of the church and chief shepherd of his flock. The Orthodox have historically seen things differently, believing that Rome's primacy was granted not by Christ, but by the councils, and then only

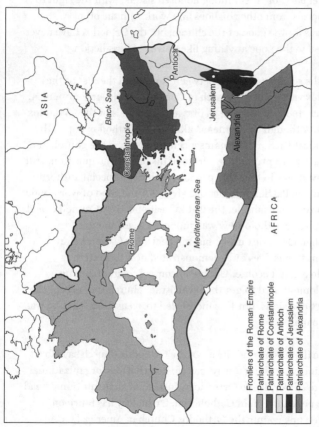

6. Map of the Christian world during the fourth and fifth centuries delineating the jurisdiction of the five patriarchates. Orthodox ecclesiology accepts the essential equality of all bishops, but since the fourth century it has also embraced the idea that the bishops of Rome, Constantinople, Alexandria, Antioch, and Jerusalem hold a special position based upon the importance of their sees.

because it was at the time capital of the empire. When the capital was moved to Constantinople, Constantinople was accorded equal dignity with Rome, although neither was given any special authority as a result of this decision. Rome was indeed "first among equals," or "first among honored sisters," with the right to hear appeals from other bishops and work with the other patriarchs for the good of the church, but the Orthodox have never conceded to the pope anything like universal jurisdiction.

When the schism occurred between Rome and the rest of the Orthodox world, the Patriarch of Constantinople, or Ecumenical Patriarch, took up the role as first among equals in the Orthodox Church. Although by no means akin to an "Orthodox pope," the Ecumenical Patriarch remains a central figure in the church and enjoys a certain primacy by virtue of his office. The question, still unresolved, is whether this primacy includes a special authority allowing the Patriarch to act decisively for the good of worldwide Orthodoxy. For example, the 2016 Great and Holy Council called by Patriarch Bartholomew was supposed to exhibit and strengthen Orthodox unity, but the decision of several churches to absent themselves only demonstrated how disunited Orthodoxy had become. Unable to compel their attendance, Bartholomew tried to get the recalcitrant churches to accept the council's decisions, but this merely led to accusations that he was being "papal."

Because there is no one "head" of the Orthodox Church save for Jesus himself, it is not always easy to flowchart the organizational structure of worldwide Orthodoxy. Instead of an institutional head like the pope in Roman Catholicism, Orthodoxy has fourteen (sixteen if one counts the Orthodox Church of America [OCA] and the Ukrainian Orthodox Church) self-governing ("autocephalous") churches, each ruled by a patriarch or metropolitan bishop. Each is free to take decisions regarding their internal affairs, but no one bishop can act on behalf of all. These churches include the following:

- Patriarchate of Constantinople;
- Patriarchate of Alexandria;
- Patriarchate of Antioch;
- Patriarchate of Jerusalem;
- Patriarchate of Moscow;
- Patriarchate of Serbia;
- Patriarchate of Romania;
- Patriarchate of Bulgaria;
- Patriarchate of Georgia;
- Church of Cyprus;
- Church of Greece;
- Church of Poland;
- Church of Albania;
- Church of the Czech Lands and Slovakia;
- Orthodox Church of America, whose autocephaly was granted by Moscow in 1970, but never recognized by the Ecumenical Patriarch; and
- Ukrainian Orthodox Church, controversially given autocephaly in 2019 by the Ecumenical Patriarchate but whose status is contested by Moscow.

The heads of these churches are all in communion with one another and recognize each other as "Orthodox," even if there are sometimes temporary disagreements because of jurisdictional disputes or disciplinary issues. The Ecumenical Patriarch remains de jure first among the bishops, although the Patriarch of Moscow has achieved a de facto primacy within Orthodoxy because of the size of his church—roughly 40 percent of the world's Orthodox Christians live in Russia. Unsurprisingly, Constantinople and Moscow are frequently at odds over their respective importance and it is not uncommon for the two sees to quarrel. In 1996 the Moscow Patriarchate broke communion with the Patriarch of Constantinople by omitting his name from the diptychs (the list of other Orthodox bishops commemorated at the liturgy). More recently, Patriarch Bartholomew's 2019 decision to grant autocephaly to the Ukrainian Orthodox Church led Moscow again to break communion, precipitating a schism between Orthodoxy's two great sees.

The Orthodox Church claims to possess the fullness of the One, Holy, Catholic, and Apostolic church. In other words, Orthodoxy believes that it has preserved the faith of Jesus Christ untainted by error or addition and for that reason views itself as the true church. The question with which the Orthodox continue to wrestle concerns the status of other Christians and whether they too have any share of the true church of Christ. Some hold that Christian groups separated from Orthodoxy may still have elements of the true church of Christ within them (for example, apostolic succession or adherence for the patristic tradition), even if they do not have them in their fullness. For this reason these Christian groups are properly "churches" with whom the Orthodox can and should engage in dialogue in order to bring them from imperfect into perfect communion with the one, true church.

The other view, which has great currency outside the United States and Western Europe, is that those who have left Orthodoxy have no relation to the true church and thus cannot be described as churches in the proper sense. Holders of this view consider these groups to be heretics (those who have embraced false teaching), schismatics (those who have broken with the church), or apostates (those who have left the faith) who must once again return to the true faith in order to find salvation. This would include not only Protestant Christians, but also Roman Catholics, toward whom many Orthodox still bear a particular animus. These individuals regard Mark of Ephesus and the other Pillars of Orthodoxy as heroes for resisting the heresies of Rome, and some have even gone so far as to condemn the Ecumenical Patriarch for his willingness to improve relations with the Catholic Church.

Despite this resistance from the more conservative elements in the church, Orthodoxy has been an active part of the ecumenical movement, working to heal Christianity's many divisions from the beginning. The 1920 encyclical of the Ecumenical Patriarchate, which called for a "league of churches" similar to the League of Nations, was the inspiration for the 1948 founding of the World Council of Churches (WCC). Relations with the Anglican church have always been particularly warm despite recent disagreements over women's ordination and certain moral teachings. The Orthodox have also worked with the Oriental Orthodox, or Coptic, churches to overcome the linguistic differences that separated them back in the fifth century, and the results of the dialogues have brought the two to the brink of restored communion.

However, in discussions of the Orthodox Church's relations with other Christians, it is the dialogue with the Roman Catholic Church that usually takes center stage. There is nothing surprising about this—Roman Catholicism is not only the single largest Christian denomination in the world with 1.2 billion believers, but also the church with whom Orthodoxy shares the most similarities. After all, they were part of the same church for more than a millennium, they both adhere to the seven ecumenical councils, both venerate the same fathers, and today there are only a few issues that keep them from full unity.

The first issue is the *filioque*, which remains in the creed of the Catholic Church despite Orthodox objections to its unilateral insertion. Theologically much has been done to move the two sides closer on understanding the procession of the Holy Spirit, but so far nothing has actually been resolved. Far more difficult has been the problem of the papacy, as the Orthodox cannot accept the Catholic teaching that the pope is universal head of the church, with an infallible teaching authority distinct from that of the councils. Recent dialogues have made a great deal of progress, especially in examining the role of the papacy during Christianity's

7. Ecumenical Patriarch Bartholomew I and Pope Francis of Rome at the Catholic Cathedral of the Holy Spirit during the pope's 2014 visit to Istanbul. Orthodox relations with the papacy, which have a long and troubled history, have greatly improved since the mid-twentieth century.

first millennium when East and West were still united, but as with the *filioque*, nothing concrete has been decided. Even so, relations between Rome and the Orthodox have improved greatly since the 1964 encounter of Patriarch Athenagoras and Pope Paul VI in Jerusalem. Formal dialogues on the theological issues continue their work while the two churches repair the fraternal bonds that once joined Christian East and West. The frequent meetings of pope and patriarch, and their common efforts on behalf of refugees, Christians in the Middle East, and the environment, underscore the growing closeness of Christianity's two largest denominations.

The Orthodox Church operates on a global scale, but for most Orthodox believers the primary point of contact with "the church" is the parish where they come together on Sundays and feast days for worship. It is on the local level, especially in the celebration of the liturgy, that the reality of the church comes alive. Led by the parish priest, who is sometimes assisted by a deacon, the Orthodox Christian encounters Christ in the midst of a community of believers. It is here that s/he can participate in the various ministries that serve either the church or the larger community. Although some of the church's ministries require a formal ordination, including those of bishop, priest, and deacon, most others do not. From the members of the choir to the outreach and hospitality committees, most Orthodox parishes are sustained largely by the efforts of those who give their time and talent to ministry in and for the church.

Chapter 9

"We no longer knew whether we were in heaven or on earth"

When non-Orthodox Christians speak about their first experience of Orthodox worship, they usually begin by describing how different it is from a Catholic or Protestant service. They might comment on its length (the Orthodox Sunday liturgy is usually twice as long as the average Catholic mass) or the frequency with which believers make the sign of the cross. Even the church building itself, with the icons that surround it and the ever-present smell of incense, strikes most Western Christians as unfamiliar and foreign. This sense of "foreignness" is increased exponentially in those Orthodox churches that have maintained the use of the Greek or Russian language, since the prayers and chants used during worship can be neither understood nor sung by visitors.

Yet for the Orthodox themselves, the church and its worship are not only familiar, but also comforting. Metropolitan Kallistos Ware, perhaps the best-known Orthodox theologian in the English-speaking world, describes his first visit to an Orthodox church in 1952: "Everything at the vigil service was in Slavonic, and so with my conscious brain I could understand not a single word. Yet as I left the church, I said to myself with a clear sense of conviction: This is where I belong; I have come home." It is perhaps this same feeling that engulfed the representatives of

Prince Vladimir of Kiev when they visited Hagia Sophia in 988—in Orthodoxy they felt like they had finally found their spiritual home.

It is hardly surprising that Vladimir's emissaries, in describing their experience, wrote that "we knew not whether we were in heaven or on earth," for this is exactly the effect Orthodox worship is designed to produce. From the moment one enters the church for the Divine Liturgy (from the Greek *leitourgia*, or "work of the people"), the believer should feel himself transported beyond time and space to the eternal worship of God that takes place in heaven, where the angels forever sing praises to the Holy Trinity. This idea, that in liturgy we accompany the angels in their eternal praise of God, is most clearly expressed in the Cherubic Hymn, sung before the gifts are presented, when the congregation sings:

> Let us, who mystically represent the Cherubim,
> And chant the thrice-holy hymn to the Life-giving Trinity,
> Set aside the cares of life
> That we may receive the King of all,
> Who comes invisibly escorted by the Divine Hosts.

Therefore, during the liturgy, Orthodox believers join with the angels and saints in this heavenly worship, enabling men and women on earth to fulfill the purpose for which humanity was originally created: to stand before God in adoration and praise. We are, when all is said and done, liturgical beings.

An understanding of this principle clarifies Orthodox liturgy greatly. For example, while the icons of the saints are undeniably beautiful and add much to the aesthetics of the church, their real purpose is to remind believers of those saints and angels who are worshipping alongside them in the heavenly court. But it is not just the sense of sight that helps transport the believer. The use of incense engages the sense of smell, while the chanting of a choir allows one to hear echoes of the angels. Even the repetition of the litanies—"Lord have mercy" is sung more than sixty times during the average Sunday service—inculcates the sense that one is engaged in something far more profound than a mere community gathering.

That said, the liturgy is also exactly that: a gathering of believers where the church becomes real and manifests itself primarily in the act of worship. Jesus said that "where two or three are gathered in my name, I am there among them" (Matt. 18:20), and this concept is very much at the heart of Orthodox thinking on the liturgy. Orthodox Christians do not gather to "witness" the liturgy, as if they were merely spectators, but instead are there to make Christ present among them by their active participation in the church's worship. It is true that sometimes this important principle gets overlooked due to the fact that most believers do not "participate" in the liturgy in the same way that Catholics and Protestants do. In Orthodox worship the priest and deacon speak most of the prayers, while the choir sings the majority of responses and various other pieces. In many churches the congregants actually say very little outside of the "Our Father" and prayers before communion, often giving the impression that they are not participating at all.

This reality, which is far from the ideal, masks the important belief in Orthodoxy that liturgy is an essentially ecclesial act—that is, it is an act of the entire church. The priest leads the congregation in prayer, yet he is not praying alone while they merely listen. Rather, the priest stands before the church in the sanctuary (the area in the church where the altar sits), facing with the people toward the East (traditionally believed to be the direction from which the day of resurrection will come), praying with them and for them and for all the world. He stands behind the *iconostasis* (the "icon-wall" that stands between the sanctuary and the rest of the church), but he is never separate from those he leads. It is true that Orthodox chant is sometimes too complicated for congregational singing, but ideally believers should be able to join in when more familiar chants are used.

Yet even when they remain silent, the Orthodox show they are participating with their bodies; the frequent prostrations and signing of the cross over one's self during the liturgy are clear signs that the believer is actively engaged. In most churches the congregation stands during most (if not all) of the liturgy, although pews have begun to appear with more frequency in the United States. In the West families usually stand or sit together, while in other parts of the Orthodox world women and men are segregated, a practice more rooted in local custom than in theology. Interestingly, in Orthodoxy it is quite common for people to move around the church even when the liturgy is in progress, lighting candles and kissing icons in order to express their faith.

The worship service regularly attended by most Orthodox Christians is the Divine Liturgy, which is the celebration of the Eucharist that takes place on Sundays and feast days. Although

8. A Russian Orthodox woman lights a candle during Christmas liturgy. Orthodox Christians frequently light candles in front of icons, both to honor the one portrayed and to symbolize the offering of one's prayers to God.

the Divine Liturgy may be celebrated on a daily basis in monasteries, Orthodoxy does not have the tradition of a daily Eucharist as became customary in the West. Also, unlike most Western churches, there are not multiple liturgies on Sundays—as a general rule, there is only one celebration of the Eucharist per day per altar.

The most frequently celebrated Eucharistic service is the Liturgy of St. John Chrysostom, which despite differences in language is common to all Orthodox churches. On ten special days throughout the year, the Liturgy of St. Basil the Great is used, although structurally the two services are not that different. Both begin with the Liturgy of Preparation (*Prothesis* in Greek, meaning "setting forth," or *Proskomidia* in Russian, meaning "the offering"), which is the preparation of the bread and wine performed by the priest behind the iconostasis. Then comes the Liturgy of the Word, which begins with several litanies (a list of prayer intentions followed by "Lord have mercy") and antiphons (psalms and responses). The "Little Entrance" then takes place, when the priest and those assisting him proceed out from behind the iconostasis, usually through one of the two "deacon doors" built into it, carrying the Book of the Gospels. After the Thrice-Holy or *Trisagion* Hymn ("Holy God, Holy Mighty, Holy Immortal, have mercy on us"), there are several readings from both the Old and New Testaments, followed by the singing of the Alleluia and the chanting of the Gospel. The priest then gives the sermon or homily (a reflection on the Gospel), after which there are three additional litanies, although in some Orthodox churches it is not uncommon for the priest to preach at the end of the service.

The Liturgy of the Faithful (the Eucharist) begins with the Cherubic Hymn and the "Great Entrance," when the priest and his assistants enter from behind the iconostasis with the offering of bread and wine. As the gifts are carried around the church, it is common for believers to bow and bless themselves as they pass. The Nicene–Constantinopolitan Creed is then sung by all before the Eucharistic prayer (*Anaphora*) begins. Historically there has been a minor dispute between Catholics and Orthodox over the exact moment of consecration (the moment the bread and wine become the body and blood of Christ): Catholics hold that it occurs during the words of institution ("This is my body…"), while the Orthodox maintain that it occurs after the *Epiklesis* ("Lord, send down your Spirit upon these gifts…"), but the reality is that the Eucharistic prayers of each church always contain both elements.

After further litanies there is the Lord's Prayer ("Our Father"), the bowing of heads, and the elevation of gifts ("The holy things are for the holy"). It is customary at this point for both the priest and the people to say a prayer before communion ("I believe, O Lord, and I confess that You are truly the Christ, the Son of the living God"), after which the priest begins distributing the gifts to the congregation. The priest places the broken and consecrated bread into the chalice; a communion spoon is then used to place a soaked piece in the mouths of those receiving. As individuals approach with arms folded, he addresses each one ("The servant of God, [NAME], partakes of the Body and Blood of Christ for the remission of sins and life eternal"). In most churches it is common for those who receive, and those not receiving, to share a piece of the *antidoron* (blessed bread), signifying fellowship. Once communion is over there is a Litany of Thanksgiving and a series of dismissal prayers before the liturgy is finally concluded.

There are a number of other liturgies in the Orthodox Church, including *orthros* (matins or morning prayer), *vespers* (evening prayer), *apodeipnon* (compline or night prayer), and *mesonyktikon* (the midnight service). The Book of Hours (*Horologion*) also contains prayers to be said at specific times throughout the day, although many of these services are only held regularly in monastic houses. The *Typikon* (the book containing the rubrics for different services throughout the year) varies slightly depending on jurisdiction, just as the *Menaion* (calendar and order of feasts) does.

Adding to this diversity is the issue of the calendar. Some Orthodox churches (in Russia and Jerusalem, for example) continue to use the calendar established by Julius Caesar (the Julian calendar) to set the dates of particular feasts, while others (Constantinople, Alexandria, Antioch) use a revised calendar aligned to the one promulgated by Pope Gregory XIII in 1582 (the Gregorian calendar). This helps explains why the Russian church celebrates Christmas on January 7, because it still uses the old Julian calendar, which is thirteen days behind the Gregorian, to calculate when December 25 occurs. In fact, the Ecumenical Patriarch's decision to adopt the revised Julian calendar led a group of "Old Calendarists" to break communion with the church of Constantinople in 1923. This division, like the "Old Believers" schism in Russia, has not yet been healed.

The Orthodox calendar revolves, like planets circling the sun, around the feast of Pascha (the feast of Christ's resurrection, also known as Easter). Yet calculating the actual date of Pascha, which was set by the Council of Nicaea, is a bit of a problem, especially as the Orthodox and the Western churches have very different ways of determining when "the first Sunday after the first full moon on or after the vernal equinox" occurs. The Orthodox Church uses the Julian calendar to set the date of the vernal equinox on March 21 (April 3 on the Gregorian calendar), which means that the Orthodox celebration of Pascha can sometimes (but not always) be several weeks later than the Catholic and Protestant observance. For example, in 2016 the West observed Easter on March 27, whereas the Orthodox did not observe the feast until May 1. However, the following year East and West celebrated Pascha on the same day, April 16, showing just how hard it can be to make any sense of the whole issue.

Pascha, for the Orthodox, is the "Feast of Feasts" for which believers begin preparing themselves several weeks in advance. Even before the start of Great Lent (the forty-day preparation period preceding Pascha), the Orthodox make themselves ready by reading a series of gospels emphasizing the theme of repentance. In the weeks immediately preceding Great Lent, Christians prepare for the Lenten fast by ridding themselves of meat ("Meat-fare Sunday") and dairy ("Cheese-Fare Sunday"). The latter Sunday is also known as Forgiveness Sunday, when it is common for Christians to ask forgiveness from everyone they have harmed during the previous year.

Great Lent itself begins on a Monday, and unlike in the West it does not include the distribution of ashes. During Lent the Orthodox keep a relatively rigorous fast that prohibits meat, fish (except shellfish), dairy products, olive oil, and alcohol. There are allowances made for age and health, and in many cases people choose to observe only certain parts of the fast. It is also common during Lent for the Liturgy of the Pre-Sanctified (a special vesper service where communion is distributed) to be celebrated during the week. On the Sundays of Great Lent the Orthodox remember particular events and saints, including:

- the Triumph of Orthodoxy—the victory over iconoclasm in 843, usually commemorated by a procession around the church with icons;

- Sunday of Gregory Palamas;

- Sunday of the Holy Cross;

- Sunday of St. John Climacus (St. John's *Ladder of Divine Ascent* describes the soul's ascent to God and the various pitfalls that can take place along the way);

- Sunday of Mary of Egypt; and

- Lazarus Saturday, which is celebrated the day before Palm/ Passion Sunday.

All of this preparation leads up to Holy Week, beginning with Palm or Passion Sunday, when it is common for palm branches or pussy willows to be distributed to the congregation in memory of Christ's triumphal entry into Jerusalem. Next comes Holy and Great

Thursday, where the church observes the institution of the Mystical (Last) Supper. The following day, Holy and Great Friday, commemorates the passion and death of Christ and is celebrated with a sobriety and silence befitting the occasion. At this service the *Epitaphios* (an embroidered cloth containing an icon of Christ being taken down from the cross) is placed on a table in the middle of the church so that it can be reverenced by the faithful. Not until the Paschal liturgy begins at midnight on Saturday does the joy of the resurrection once again fill the air, with candlelight processions around the church and the Paschal *troparion* (hymn) sung by all—"Christ is risen from the dead, trampling down death by death and upon those in the tombs bestowing life!" The Paschal greeting ("Christ is risen!" "Truly He is risen!") is then exchanged, and at the conclusion of the service, which is often just before daybreak, it is common for the congregation to gather and feast together on all the foods they have avoided since the beginning of the fast.

Along with Pascha, which remains the centerpiece of the Orthodox liturgical year, there are also the "The Twelve Great Feasts," which include:

- Palm/Passion Sunday—the Sunday before Pascha;

- the Ascension—forty days after Pascha, commemorating the ascent of Christ into heaven;

- Pentecost—fifty days after Pascha, celebrating the descent of the Holy Spirit upon the apostles;

- the Nativity of the *Theotokos*—observed on September 8, this is the first feast of the Orthodox liturgical year, which begins September 1;

- the Elevation of the Holy Cross—observed on September 14, the anniversary of the day that St. Helen found the true cross in Jerusalem;

- the Presentation of the *Theotokos*—observed on November 21, this celebrates the tradition that Mary herself was dedicated in the Temple by her parents, Anna and Joachim;

- the Nativity of the Lord—observed on December 25, more commonly known as Christmas;

- the Theophany of the Lord—observed on January 6, it celebrates the baptism of Christ and the revelation of God as Trinity; it is the usual practice on this day for water to be blessed;

- the Presentation of the Lord—observed on February 2, sometimes called Candlemas in the West, it commemorates Jesus's presentation in the Temple and the prophesies of Simeon and Anna;

- the Annunciation—observed on March 25, this celebrates the angel's announcement to Mary that she was to conceive a child by the Holy Spirit;

- the Transfiguration—observed on August 6, it celebrates the revelation of Jesus in his divine glory to his apostles on Mount Tabor; and

- the Dormition of the *Theotokos*—observed on August 15, it marks Mary's "falling asleep" surrounded by the apostles.

9. Greek Orthodox swimmer Nicos Solis kisses a wooden cross during the Feast of the Theophany in 2017. The feast celebrates the baptism of Christ in the Jordan River, and it is usually accompanied by the blessing of water and subsequent immersion of the faithful.

Many of these feasts are preceded by fasts and periods of preparation (including the Christmas and Dormition fasts), as are some of the other holy days in the Orthodox calendar (for example, the Apostles' fast). Another important feast, especially in Russia, is the Feast of St. Nicholas (December 6), commemorating the model bishop whose charitable outreach has made him a particular favorite among the Orthodox. His relics, which were translated (moved) to Bari during the eleventh century, continue to attract thousands of Orthodox pilgrims, and in 2017 millions lined the streets of Moscow and St. Petersburg to see them when, thanks to the intervention of Pope Francis, they were displayed in Russia for the first time.

Chapter 10
The mysteries

The Orthodox Church has blessings and ceremonies for every occasion, from the blessing of a bell (bells are usually named and anointed with oil) to the rite of blessing cheese and eggs. In each of these ceremonies the church asks for special graces to come upon the object or event so that through them Christ may be made more present in the world. For the Orthodox it is not a matter of taking an object and somehow separating it from the rest of world by making it holy. Instead, it is the consecration of one object for the purpose of making all things holy and showing forth God's presence in all of creation.

Among the various rites of the church, seven have taken on a special significance, because in these "sacraments" or "mysteries" Christ is experienced and encountered in a unique way. The numbering of these sacraments was essentially borrowed from the West, although the theology behind them remains distinctively Orthodox. In each the church takes ordinary materials—water, bread, oil—and prays that Christ may be manifested through them so that the believer comes to feel the presence of Christ in a profound and meaningful way. This idea, that the eye sees something common, while the eyes of faith see something else, explains why the Orthodox refer to these ceremonies as "mysteries." To the unbeliever the sacraments of the church are little more than beautiful ceremonies. To the Orthodox Christian they are encounters with God.

The first sacrament, which joins the believer to Christ and the Christian community, is baptism (from the Greek *baptizo*, meaning "plunging" or "washing"). Not only is the individual joined to Christ, dying and rising with him to new life (Rom. 6:4), but he is also cleansed of sin and made pure, an act symbolized by the use of a white garment whereby one "puts on Christ" (Gal. 3:27). The idea of ritual cleansing was very much part of Jewish tradition and was central to the ministry of John the Forerunner (also known as John the Baptist). Christ himself accepted baptism at John's hands and in the Gospel of Matthew told his apostles to "go therefore and make disciples of all nations, baptizing them in the name of the Father and of the Son and of the Holy Spirit" (Matt. 28:19). Because this command has such a clear biblical warrant, almost all Christian churches continue to practice baptism, even if the Orthodox tend to do it a little differently than Western churches.

First, unlike most Christian denominations in the West, Orthodoxy continues to practice baptism by full-body immersion; candidates for the sacrament do not have water poured over their heads, but are rather completely immersed into the font. Because most Orthodox baptisms take place during infancy this is usually not a problem, but the logistics of adult baptisms can be a bit more challenging. The second big difference is that in Orthodoxy the three sacraments of initiation (baptism, chrismation, and Eucharist) are given at the same time, which means that immediately after their baptism new Christians are anointed and receive communion, even if they are only weeks old. This was the custom of the ancient church, and although the churches of the West later divided the three sacraments—giving "first communion" to those age seven and older and celebrating confirmation during adolescence—some Catholic theologians have begun to argue in favor of restoring the older practice.

The second sacrament, usually celebrated along with baptism, is chrismation, known more often in the West as confirmation. In this sacrament believers are anointed with chrism (perfumed oil) in order to seal them with the Holy Spirit and strengthen them for the Christian life. The priest anoints the forehead to sanctify one's thoughts, the chest to sanctify one's heart, the eyes, ears, and lips to sanctify one's senses, and the hands and feet so that one will always walk in the ways of the Lord. Normally part of the baptismal ritual, in most (but certainly not all) Orthodox churches converts can be received into Orthodoxy by chrismation, provided they have already received baptism in another Christian denomination.

The third sacrament, and by far the most important of them all, is the Eucharist (from the Greek *eucharistein*, meaning "to give thanks"). The sacrament itself is understood not only as the great act of thanksgiving for what God has done for humankind in Christ, but also as a sacrifice in which Jesus, whom the Father gave to us, is offered back to God as well. This is why during the liturgy the priest says, "Thine own of Thine own, we offer to Thee, on behalf of all, and for all"—in Orthodox thought Christ himself is offered upon the altar for the benefit of all humanity, both living and deceased. The gifts, which began as bread and wine, become, by the prayers of the priest and the invocation of the Holy Spirit, the very body and blood of Jesus Christ.

This last affirmation raises an issue that has divided Christians for almost five hundred years: the exact nature of Christ's presence in the Eucharist. During the Reformation many Protestants began to teach that Christ became only symbolically present in the bread and wine or that Christ's presence could only be understood spiritually. In response, at the Council of Trent (1545–1563), the Roman Catholic Church reaffirmed the true and substantial presence of Christ in the Eucharist, teaching that during the mass there was a "transubstantiation" (change in substance) in the bread and wine so that it was no longer bread and wine, but rather the true body and blood of Christ. The Protestants, although they could never quite agree among themselves on a position, almost universally rejected the Catholic teaching on transubstantiation, and most continue to do so today.

Orthodoxy was not originally part of this debate, and it was only when Protestants and Catholics began making their way east in the sixteenth and seventeenth centuries that the Orthodox felt the need to clarify their own stance. When it did, Orthodoxy chose to adopt the language of Roman Catholicism, teaching in many catechisms of the period that transubstantiation was also a doctrine of the Orthodox Church. Yet in the twentieth century many within Orthodoxy became uncomfortable with this development, arguing that while the Catholic teaching was not necessarily wrong, it was not truly reflective of the Orthodox tradition. Orthodoxy has long acknowledged that there is a real change in the bread and wine and that Christ does become truly present upon the altar—the liturgy itself prays that God will "make this bread the precious Body of Your Christ, and that which is in this Cup, the precious Blood of Your Christ, changing them by Your Holy Spirit"—but the Orthodox believe that it is not possible to define exactly how all this happens. The Catholic teaching, in trying to do just that, seemed to go beyond what is permitted.

The idea that in receiving the very body and blood of Christ we achieve a unique union or "communion," both with God and one another, is central to Orthodox thinking on the Eucharist. Communion with God, the very reason for which we were created, is experienced in a real way, and the church becomes "most authentically itself" when it gathers to make Christ present in its midst. Because this idea of union with God and the church is so important, the Orthodox practice what is often referred to as "closed communion"—that is, they do not allow Christians who are not "in communion" with the Orthodox Church (namely, Catholics and Protestants) to receive the consecrated elements. While some outsiders might see this as a lack of hospitality, for the Orthodox it is imperative that the sharing of Eucharistic communion reflects a unity of faith and love that already exists. That said, there have been moments in the history of the Orthodox Church when, because of extraordinary circumstances or dire need (for example, in the Gulag during the Soviet persecutions), sacramental sharing with the non-Orthodox was implicitly allowed.

The sacrament of reconciliation or confession is the means by which all sins committed after one's baptism are forgiven. Confessions are usually heard in the open in front of the iconostasis; both the priest and the penitent stand beside a table holding a cross, an icon of Christ, and the Scriptures. Orthodoxy, in both the setting of the sacrament and its prayers, emphasizes that God is the one offering forgiveness; the priest is "but a witness, bearing testimony before Him of all the things which you have to say." After confessing his or her sins the penitent kneels or bows before the priest, who places his stole (*epitrachilion*) on their head before saying the prayer of absolution. Unlike Roman Catholicism, where the priest grants absolution ("I absolve you of your sins"), the usual formula in the Greek Orthodox Church is "May God forgive you in this world and the next." The Russian formula is much closer to its Catholic counterpart ("May our Lord God and Savior Jesus Christ, through his grace and love towards mankind forgive you my child all your sins and I the unworthy priest through the power given to me, absolve and forgive all your sins").

The fourth sacrament, anointing of the sick, also known as Holy Unction, reminds Christians that Christ remains present to them through the ministry of the church, especially during times of physical, emotional, or spiritual pain. The basis for this sacrament is found in the Epistle of James: "Are any among you sick? They should call for the elders of the church and have them pray over them, anointing them with oil in the name of the Lord" (James 5:14). After several New Testament readings, gospels, and prayers, all of which are devoted to healing, the priest anoints the body with holy oil, here used as a sign of God's strength, just as it is in chrismation. Also associated with the forgiveness of sins, this sacrament is oftentimes misunderstood, even by the Orthodox themselves, to be the "last rites" of the Orthodox Church. In fact, it can be celebrated at any time the believer feels the need for Christ's healing strength, regardless of age or condition.

Marriage finds its basis in the act of creation, when God created Eve from Adam's rib so that she would be "bone of my bones and flesh of my flesh." This is why, according to Scripture, "man leaves his father and his mother and clings to his wife, and they become one flesh" (Gen. 2:23–24). Today the church continues to bless this union of man and woman in the sacrament of marriage, which consists of two separate rituals often performed at the same time. The first is the Office of Betrothal, which takes place at the entrance of the church building and includes the blessing and exchange of rings. The second is the Office of Crowning, where the priest places crowns, oftentimes made of flowers but sometimes made of gold, on the heads of the couple. These are supposed to be both crowns of joy and crowns of martyrdom, because every marriage includes a dying-to-self for the good of the other. At the end of the service the couple drinks wine from the same cup, which not only recalls Jesus's miracle at the wedding at Cana (John 2:1-11), but also symbolizes that the newly married now share a common life.

Orthodoxy usually permits inter-Christian marriage, albeit unenthusiastically, provided the non-Orthodox party has received a valid baptism. However, marriages to non-Christians are generally forbidden and place the Orthodox party outside the sacramental life of the church, meaning that he or she cannot receive Eucharist or the other sacraments. The Orthodox Church, while maintaining that marriages are ideally indissoluble, recognizes that the reality of human sin makes it impossible for some couples to keep this lifelong commitment. In such cases the church, with great sadness, recognizes the reality of divorce and will even perform second or third marriages. However, these latter ceremonies are far more subdued affairs than the first, often including penitential prayers.

The seventh sacrament is Holy Orders, where the bishop, by the laying on of hands, ordains a man to service in the church. Although there are minor orders in the church (offices such as reader and sub-deacon, each of which has certain assigned roles during the liturgy), the three major orders are deacon, priest, and bishop. Deacons (from the Greek *diákonos*, or "service") assist the priest during the liturgy and chant many of the litanies. Priests perform the sacraments and are chiefly responsible for the celebration of the Eucharist. Unlike the Roman Catholic Church, the Orthodox Church permits married men to be ordained as priests and deacons, and today most parish clergy are married with children. In many Greek and Russian communities the priest's wife, who often plays an important role in the life of the parish, is addressed as *Presbytera* ("Elder") or *Matushka* ("Little Mother"), which are the feminine forms for the priests' own titles—*Presbyteros* and *Batiushka*. However, all marriages must take place prior to ordination; once deacons and priests are ordained they cannot marry, even if they are widowed. Bishops are always celibate—either widowers or monks—and are traditionally chosen by the local clergy or picked by the governing synod of his particular church. Even in the latter, there is a role for popular consent; during each ordination in the Orthodox Church, the people agree to the candidate's new ministry by yelling "*Axios!*" or "[He is] worthy!"

Orthodox clergy traditionally wear long black cassocks and usually (but not necessarily) beards. The *kalimavkion* (hat) worn by most Orthodox clergy can vary in color depending on the church. Monks of all jurisdictions wear a *kalimavkion* with a veil. Priestly vestments used for liturgy include the *sticharion* (tunic), *epitrachelion* (stole), *epimanikia* (cuffs), and *phelonion* (chasuble). For liturgical functions bishops typically wear miters (resembling crowns) and carry pastoral staffs, which symbolize their role as spiritual shepherds. These staffs are often topped with two snakes facing the cross, harkening back to the words of Jesus: "See, I am sending you out like sheep into the midst of wolves; so be wise as serpents and innocent as doves" (Matt. 10:16). Bishops also wear the *omophorion*, which is a strip of cloth decorated with a series of crosses and worn over the neck and shoulders. Because it is symbolic of his pastoral authority, like the pallium worn by Catholic archbishops, anyone serving under his jurisdiction is said to be "under his omophorion."

Whether given at infancy or in infirmity, the Orthodox conviction is that Christ himself is encountered in each of the seven mysteries, and it is he who provides believers with the grace needed for their particular ministry or state of life. For the Orthodox sacraments are not merely ceremonies or celebrations that mark important milestones in one's Christian journey; rather, they are manifestations of Christ's ongoing presence in the world, even in material objects as common as water, bread, and oil, strengthening believers in times of need and preparing them for the journey ahead.

Chapter 11
Orthodoxy and the modern world

The twentieth and twenty-first centuries have been times of great upheaval for the Orthodox, bringing not only persecutions and mass emigrations, but also rebirth and the possibility of new growth. There is reason for pessimism: At the beginning of the twentieth century, 20 percent of the world's Christians were Orthodox, while at the beginning of the twenty-first, that number stood at 12 percent. Orthodox Christians in Syria, Egypt, and Palestine confront a new era of persecution as the victims of civil war, Islamist terror, and political turmoil. In the face of church bombings and constant threats, thousands of Christians have decided to flee their historic homelands, leaving the future of Orthodoxy in the Middle East in doubt. Yet there is also reason for hope—Orthodoxy in Africa has boomed, with the Ethiopian Church (an Oriental Orthodox community) gaining more than thirty million believers during the twentieth century. During the 1990s, after emerging from years of persecution under the communists, the Russian Orthodox Church, often with the financial support of the government, experienced a renaissance, building churches and serving as a key player in the development of post-Soviet Russian identity.

In the United States and Western Europe the fortunes of the Orthodox have been mixed. They do not face outright persecution, but neither do they receive the support of a traditionally Orthodox culture. In fact, as Western society itself becomes less Christian, both demographically and culturally, the Orthodox, like other Christians in the West, are increasingly forced to live in a world where religion is either a matter of indifference or the subject of derision. There has been a precipitous rise in the number of individuals identifying as "non-religious" or "non-affiliated," and rates of church attendance have plummeted since the 1950s. Even in countries like Russia, where more than 70 percent of the population self-identifies as Orthodox, less than 10 percent actually attend church on a regular basis (once a month or more), and attendance rates among men are half that. Interestingly, while the Orthodox population of the United States is much smaller (0.5 percent of the population), rates of church attendance are much higher, with more than 30 percent attending weekly. Still, the reality remains that the Orthodox in the West live in societies that no longer support religious belief and practice as they did only a few generations ago.

Nowhere is this reality more apparent than in the "culture wars" that have dominated the headlines since the late twentieth century. No longer shaped exclusively by the Judeo-Christian tradition, the views of Western society on certain moral issues have diverged sharply from established Christian teaching. Debates over the legality of abortion, same-sex marriage, and the place of religion in the public square have forced Christians to take sides, often revealing sharp divisions between church authorities and the opinions of their congregants. The Orthodox are not immune from this phenomenon. According to Pew Research, despite the strong opposition of the bishops to abortion, roughly half of all Orthodox Christians in the United States believe it should be legal in most cases. Although the bishops also oppose same-sex marriage, less than half of the Orthodox in America agree with them, with most instead supporting the idea of marriage equality.

Figures like these have naturally caused alarm in some circles, especially among Catholic and Protestant converts who came to Orthodoxy precisely because it was perceived to be the more "traditional" church. Many of these individuals have embraced the so-called Benedict Option, maintaining that society has become so hostile to Christianity that the only option left is to retreat, preserving the true faith in small committed communities while the world around them goes its own way. Although it is certainly not the majority view, there are ultraconservative elements in Greece, Russia, and Eastern Europe who believe that Orthodoxy in the West has lost its way and is beyond redemption. For example, in 1998, Bishop Nikon of Yekaterinburg ordered books by Alexander Schmemann and John Meyendorff, two of America's best-known Orthodox theologians, to be burned as heretical, an act for which he was later censured.

10. Orthodox bishops from around the world gather for the Opening Session of the Holy and Great Council of the Orthodox Church at Crete. Preparations for a council began in the early part of the twentieth century, yet it did not meet until 2016, and even then, several local churches declined to participate.

Tensions among Orthodoxy's various factions were on full display at the Great and Holy Council held on Crete in 2016. The chief issue of dispute was whether other Christian bodies (especially the Roman Catholic Church) were "churches" in a proper sense or whether they were simply schismatic groups that had cut themselves off from the one true church by breaking with Orthodoxy. Several Orthodox churches either refused to attend the council or rejected the draft documents based on the original wording, which seemed to embrace the former position. Eventually a compromise was reached, recognizing that the "Orthodox Church accepts the historical name of other non-Orthodox Christian churches and confessions that are not in communion with her." Simply put, the council taught that these other groups may or may not be actual "churches," but it was agreed that most people describe them as such. Even that was too much for some, as they wanted to see the wholesale denunciation of ecumenism as a heresy and rejected the slightest suggestion that Orthodoxy had anything to learn from a dialogue with heretics. The council, to their dismay, not only upheld the Orthodox commitment to the ecumenical movement, but also condemned "all efforts to break the unity of the church...under the pretext of maintaining or allegedly defending true Orthodoxy."

Alongside the ideological split within Orthodoxy remain the ever-present ethnic and jurisdictional conflicts. The churches of Antioch and Jerusalem severed communion in 2014 over the jurisdiction of Qatar, and disputes between Constantinople and Moscow over Estonia led to a brief schism in 1996. Ukraine has been a particular sore spot in recent decades, as many in the country (including both the president and the Parliament) began campaigning for the creation of an independent church outside the jurisdiction of the Moscow Patriarchate. In 2019, Ecumenical Patriarch Bartholomew finally granted their request, issuing a *tomos* of autocephaly for the newly created Ukrainian Orthodox Church. Moscow, which saw this as an uncanonical and politically motivated effort to alienate the Ukrainian church from its "mother," quickly responded by breaking communion with the Church of Constantinople, precipitating a schism that has yet to be healed. The struggle for Ukraine is not just political, but also religious.

Debates about the role of women in the church, especially after the Anglicans began ordaining women priests in 1976, forced both the Catholic and Orthodox churches to re-examine their two-thousand-year-old tradition of an all-male priesthood. Whereas the Vatican has issued two strongly worded statements on the impossibility of admitting women to the Roman Catholic priesthood (*Inter Insigniores* in 1976 and *Ordinatio Sacerdotalis* in 1994), Orthodoxy has kept relatively quiet on the matter, at least on an official level. Orthodox theologians have engaged the question, and although no decisions on the matter have been taken, nothing akin to the Vatican prohibitions has been offered by the hierarchy.

This last fact is interesting because, since the late twentieth century, several churches have begun debating the possibility of restoring the female diaconate, arguing that this ancient office—there is evidence of deaconesses in both Scripture and the early church—is part of the Tradition and should be restored. In 1998, a Pan-Orthodox Consultation on Rhodes had left open that possibility, although no further advances were made until February 2017, when the Patriarch of Alexandria blessed (but did not ordain) five nuns in the Congo to serve as deaconesses, just a few short months after his church had decided to reintroduce the office. Whether other Orthodox jurisdictions will follow suit is unclear, which means that for the present it is still an isolated case.

If Orthodoxy is perceived by some to be behind the times in dealing with the problems of the modern world, at least on one score it has been ahead of the curve—and that is care for the environment. Ecumenical Patriarch Bartholomew, nicknamed

"The Green Patriarch" for his advocacy of environmental issues, has spent years stressing the need for Christians to exercise responsible stewardship over the natural world. On many occasions he has linked care of the environment with our care for others, asking Christians to understand that "a crime against nature is a crime against ourselves and sin against God. For human beings...to destroy the biological diversity of God's creation; for human beings to degrade the integrity of the earth by causing changes in its climate, by stripping the earth of its natural forests or destroying its wetlands; for human beings to contaminate the earth's waters, its land, its air, and its life—these are sins." In fact, when Pope Francis of Rome issued his own encyclical on the environment in 2015 (*Laudato Si*, or "On care for our common home"), he dedicated it to the Patriarch, whose speeches and writings on the subject were amply footnoted. Francis even took the unprecedented step of inviting Metropolitan John Zizioulas of Pergamon, representing the Patriarch, to speak at the encyclical's promulgation.

Concerning issues of sexual morality, Orthodoxy often finds itself sharing the views of the Catholic Church, although the lack of a centralized Orthodox teaching authority similar to the Vatican's can sometimes obscure this fact. The Orthodox Church is unambiguously pro-life and has been a vocal opponent of legalized abortion both in the United States and abroad. At the annual March for Life in Washington, DC, the Orthodox Church is always well represented, with bishops, clergy, and laity among the marchers. In 2013, the Orthodox bishops of the United States issued a statement reaffirming that "the sacrament of marriage consists in the union of a man and a woman," but at the same time urged that "persons with homosexual orientation are to be cared for with the same mercy and love that is bestowed on all of humanity by our Lord Jesus Christ."

The one area where Orthodoxy differs somewhat from Roman Catholicism concerns artificial birth control, which Pope Paul VI's

1968 encyclical *Humanae Vitae* condemned as contrary to the inherently procreative nature of the sexual act. In August of that year Patriarch Athenagoras of Constantinople wrote to the pope that he was "in total agreement" with the encyclical's position, and yet this view was not universally shared. Today a variety of responses to birth control coexist within the Orthodox Church, ranging from outright condemnation to the view that such matters are best left to the couple in consultation with their spiritual advisors.

Demographically, the number of Orthodox Christians around the world is usually estimated at 250 to 300 million. Of these, more than 100 million belong to the Russian Orthodox Church, which after decades of state-sponsored atheism in the Soviet Union, emerged as a strong voice in the development of a post-communist national identity. This has brought with it an entirely new set of challenges, including debates about church–state separation and the potential exploitation of the church by national leaders for their own political ends. In Russia the Patriarch of Moscow is frequently seen interacting with President Putin during important religious feasts and state occasions, and the church's statements on the situation in Ukraine often echo the views of the government. This has created the impression that the church is being exploited by Russia's political leaders and has become a de facto arm of the government. True or not, debates about the role of Orthodoxy in Russian society are likely to continue, especially given the privileged place the church has been granted in Russia relative to other faiths.

In the United States, Orthodox Christianity remains a small but influential voice in the public square, its increased visibility largely the work of Orthodox seminaries and intellectual centers branching out into the wider world. St. Vladimir's Seminary in New York has a very active publishing division, and Fordham University's Orthodox Christian Studies Center has organized conferences and lectures on many contemporary social issues.

Orthodox theologians are regular participants at the American Academy of Religion (AAR) and meet annually as part of the Orthodox Theological Society of America (OTSA). The establishment of the International Orthodox Theological Association (IOTA) in 2017 created another outlet through which American theologians can share their work and also learn from scholars in other parts of the Orthodox world.

Too often written off as a relic of the past, Orthodox Christianity remains as vibrant and relevant today as it was during the age of the Caesars. For two millennia it has survived persecutions, schisms, and the rise and fall of empires, all the while preserving its ancient faith and bringing it to peoples throughout the world. Having achieved so much, it is easy to see why many, even among the Orthodox, are tempted to keep looking backward—to see Orthodoxy exclusively in terms of its glorious past. Yet Orthodoxy is not a museum piece or an artifact to be preserved under glass as a reminder of a bygone age. Orthodox Christianity is instead a living, breathing entity, like all life capable of evolution and growth. Today it provides millions of Christians throughout the world with their spiritual home and continues to shape world events, especially in places like Ukraine and the Holy Land. It cannot and should not be so easily dismissed.

Glossary

Akathist Hymn: a popular Marian hymn of the Orthodox Church

antidoron: blessed bread often given at Divine Liturgy to those not
   receiving communion

apostle: "one who is sent on a mission"; used to refer to the twelve
   close followers of Jesus, or can also be used to describe the larger
   group of followers (like Paul and Barnabas) who went out on
   missions to spread Christ's message

apostolic succession: the claim that a particular bishop's office or
   teachings can be traced back to the apostles

autocephalous: self-governing; usually refers to one of the fourteen
   recognized self-governing Orthodox churches; the self-governing
   status of both the Orthodox Church of America (OCA) and the
   Ukrainian Orthodox Church remains subject to debate

azymes: unleavened bread; the Western church's use of azymes in the
   Eucharist was among the reasons for the schism with the Eastern
   church

baptism: from the Greek *baptizo* meaning "plunging" or "washing";
   sacrament by which the believer is joined to Christ and the
   Christian community

bishop: ordained minister who has authority over a given territory
   called a diocese

Cappadocian fathers: collectively refers to Basil "the Great" of
   Caesarea (d. 379), Gregory of Nyssa (d. 395), and Gregory "the
   Theologian" of Nazianzus (d. 390)

chotki (or *komboskini*): beaded rope often used in conjunction with the Jesus Prayer

chrismation: sacrament in which the believer is anointed with chrism (oil) and sealed with the Holy Spirit

consensus patrum: "consensus of the fathers"; criteria often used to judge the correctness of a church teaching

coryphaeus: "choir-master"; usually describes Peter's role within the circle of apostles

deacon: from the Greek *diákonos*, "service"; ordained minister who assists the priest during the liturgy and serves the needs of the church

Deesis: an image of Christ with Mary and John the Forerunner (John the Baptist) standing on either side of him

Divine Liturgy: from the Greek *leitourgia*, "work of the people"; this is the regular form of Sunday eucharistic worship of the Orthodox Church

Eastern Catholic Churches: Orthodox who entered communion with Rome in exchange for the ability to maintain their ancient customs; also called "uniates," although this term is now considered derogatory

economia: "economy" or "management"; principle within Orthodoxy that acknowledges that church authorities can and should apply canon law for the greater spiritual good

ecumenical councils: a gathering of the whole church; usually refers to the first seven councils held from 325 to 787

Ecumenical Patriarch: the Patriarch of Constantinople

episcopos: "elder"; original Greek term for the leader of the local church community (i.e., the bishop)

Epitaphios: an embroidered cloth showing an icon of Christ being taken down from the cross

essence–energy distinction: belief explicated by Gregory Palamas that there is a distinction between the hidden essence of God and his uncreated energies experienced in prayer

ethnarch: head of a nation under the Ottoman Empire

ethnophyletism: from the Greek "nation"; the heresy that attempts to divide Orthodox Christians into national or ethnic groups

Eucharist: from the Greek *eucharistein*, "to give thanks"; central sacrament of the church in which bread and wine are changed into Christ's body and blood in order to be received by the believer

evangelion: "good news" or gospel

excommunication: the judgment that one is out of communion with the church

extra ecclesiam nulla salus: "outside the church there is no salvation"

fathers of the church: bishops and teachers of the early Christian centuries, but sometimes used also to refer to later influential figures and teachers

filioque: "and the son"; refers to the Western belief, later inserted into the Creed, that the Holy Spirit eternally proceeds from both the Father "and the Son"

gnosticism: early church heresy that claimed to be in possession of "secret knowledge" not available to all believers

Great Lent: forty-day preparation period for Pascha, involving fasting, prayer, and almsgiving

Hagia Sophia: "Holy Wisdom"; name of the church that served as the center of Orthodox life in Constantinople until 1453

heresy: incorrect faith

hesychasm: "silence"; the belief of certain Athonite monks that one can experience God as light during prayer

holy fools: saints whose erratic behavior is a witness to the "foolishness of the gospel"

homoousios: "same substance"; refers to the teaching of Nicaea that Jesus is the same substance as the Father and thus also God

Horologion: Book of Hours

iconoclasts: "smashers of images"; those who attacked the church's use of icons as violations of the first commandment

iconodules: "savers of images" (or iconophiles, or "lovers of images"); those who defended the church's use of icons and were ultimately vindicated in 843

iconostasis: "icon-wall"; usually separates the sanctuary from the main body of an Orthodox church

Jesus Prayer: "Lord Jesus Christ, Son of God, have mercy on me, a sinner"

kalimavkion: hat worn by most Orthodox clergy

lapsi: those who gave in and worshipped the emperor during the early persecutions

latria: "worship" given to God alone; usually contrasted to the *proskynesis* or "reverence" given to icons

lex orandi lex credendi: "The rule of prayer is the rule of belief"

Liturgy of St. John Chrysostom: most frequently celebrated Eucharistic liturgy of the Orthodox Church

messiah: "anointed one" or "Christ"

Mount Athos: the "Holy Mountain"; small peninsula in Greece that has served as the home of Eastern monasticism since the ninth century

mysteries: another term for the sacraments; one of the seven ceremonies of the Orthodox Church wherein Christ is experienced and encountered in a unique way

Nicene–Constantinopolitan Creed: Creed used by most major Christian churches; the Western addition of the *filioque* to the Creed is among the reasons given for the schism

"Old Believers": also **"Old Ritualists"**: those Russians who continue to reject the 1652 liturgical reforms of Patriarch Nikon

Omophorion: a strip of cloth symbolizing a bishop's pastoral authority; it is usually decorated with a series of crosses and worn over the neck and shoulders

Oriental Orthodox: also Copts; Christians in Egypt and Syria who refused to acknowledge the Council of Chalcedon in 451

orthodox: literally "correct belief" or "correct worship" (from the Greek *orthos* and *doxa*), but more often used to mean "the correct faith"

Panagia: "all-holy"; title for Mary

Pascha: also called Easter, it is the "feast of feasts" that celebrates Jesus's resurrection

patriarch: title originally given to the bishops of Rome, Constantinople, Alexandria, Antioch, and Jerusalem; today it is also used by other Orthodox hierarchs (e.g., Patriarch of Moscow)

patristics: study of the church fathers

Pedalion: "Rudder"; the most widely used canonical collection in the Orthodox Church

pentarchy: refers to the five sees (Rome, Constantinople, Alexandria, Antioch, and Jerusalem) who acted together in the ancient church as a type of "executive governing board"

perichoresis: the mutual indwelling of the persons within the Trinity without any sort of confusion among those "qualities" that make them who they are

philanthropia: "love of humanity" shown by the Father that should be reflected in people's treatment of one another

pope: "father"; title given to both the Bishop of Rome and the Bishop of Alexandria

priest: ordained minister who performs the sacraments and is chiefly responsible for the celebration of the Eucharist

primacy: the idea that certain bishops have been granted a "first-ness" among their otherwise coequal peers

proskynesis: "reverence" given to icons; usually contrasted to *latria* or "worship" given to God alone

Russian Orthodox Church Outside Russia (ROCOR): church-in-exile established after the Russian Revolution because it believed the Russian church had been co-opted by the communists

sobornorst: also synodality; the principle that the mind of the church is best expressed in a synod or council

starets: elder or spiritual father; in Russia, the *starets* is often thought to have the ability to heal or prophesy

sylites: saints who lived atop tall pillars

synergeia: "synergy"; the belief that free will and divine grace work harmoniously

taxis: "order"; the idea that although there is an essential equality between bishops there is nevertheless an order to them, giving some a certain primacy

theosis: deification; the belief of the Orthodox that humanity's destiny is to become more like God

Theotokos: "God-bearer" or "Mother of God"; title granted to Mary at the Council of Ephesus in 431

Tradition: the faith received by the Apostles, handed down over two millennia, and lived out in the daily life of the church; the sum total of the church's lived experience

Trinity: the central Christian belief that there is one divine essence shared by three persons—Father, Son, and Holy Spirit—and that these three persons are fully divine, coequal and coeternal

***Trisagion* Hymn:** "Thrice Holy Hymn"; "Holy God, Holy Mighty, Holy Immortal, have mercy on us"

Triumph of Orthodoxy: celebrated on the first Sunday of Great Lent, it commemorates the victory over iconoclasm in 843

***troparion*:** hymn

***Typikon*:** book containing the rubrics for different services throughout the year

References

Abbreviations

ACW = Ancient Christian Writers
ANF = Ante-Nicene Fathers
FC = Fathers of the Church
NPNF = Nicene and Post-Nicene Fathers
PG = Patrologia Graeca
PL = Patrologia Latina

Chapter 1: "In the beginning"

Ambrose of Milan, *Sermon against Auxentius*, 35–36; NPNF
   2.10.436.

Chapter 2: Byzantines and Franks

John of Damascus, *On the Divine Images* 1.14,16; John of Damascus,
   On the Divine Images, trans. David Anderson (Crestwood, NY: St.
   Vladimir's Seminary Press, 1980), 21, 23.
Theodore the Studite, *Epistle* 1.23; PG 99:1017–1021.
Theodosius of the Kiev Caves, *Letter to Izyaslav Yaroslavich, Grand
   Prince of Kiev*, quoted in Hilarion Alfeyev, *Orthodox Christianity*,
   vol. 1, trans. Basil Bush (Crestwood, NY: St. Vladimir's Seminary
   Press, 2011), 114–115.

Patriarch Joseph I of Constantinople, quoted in Aristeides Papadakis, *Crisis in Byzantium: The Filioque Controversy in the Patriarchate of Gregory II of Cyprus* (Crestwood, NY: St. Vladimir's Seminary Press, 1996), 21.

Chapter 3: Constantinople and Moscow

Philotheus of Pskov, Letter to Grand Duke Vasili III, quoted in John Meyendorff, *Rome, Constantinople, Moscow: Historical and Theological Studies* (Crestwood, NY: St. Vladimir's Seminary Press, 1998), 136.

Chapter 5: Sources of Orthodox thought

Jaroslav Pelikan, *The Vindication of Tradition: 1983 Jefferson Lecture in the Humanities* (New Haven, CT: Yale University Press, 1984), 65.
Canons of the Council of Trent in Norman Tanner, *Decrees of the Ecumenical Councils*, vol. 2 (Washington, DC: Georgetown University Press, 1990), 663.

Chapter 6: "I believe"

Gregory of Nyssa, *Life of Moses* 1.46–47; Gregory of Nyssa, *Life of Moses*, trans. Abraham Malherbe and Everett Ferguson, Classics of Western Spirituality (Mahwah, NJ: Paulist Press, 1978), 43.
Gregory of Nazianzus, *Oration* 28.4; Gregory of Nazianzus, *On God and Christ: The Five Theological Orations and Two Letters to Cledonius*, trans. Lionel Wickham and Frederick Williams (Crestwood, NY: St. Vladimir's Seminary Press, 2002), 30.
Gregory of Nazianzus, *Oration* 29.11; Gregory of Nazianzus, *On God and Christ*, 79.
John of Damascus, *An Exact Exposition of the Orthodox Faith* 1.1; John of Damascus, *Writings*, trans. Frederic Chase, FC 37 (Washington, DC: Catholic University of America Press, 1958), 166.
John of Damascus, *An Exact Exposition of the Orthodox Faith* 2.2; John of Damascus, *Writings*, 205.
Maximos the Confessor, *Diversa capita ad theologiam et oeconomiam spectantia deque virtute ac vitio*, 4; GEH Palmer, Philip Sherrard, and Kallistos Ware, eds. *The Philokalia*, vol. 2 (London: Faber and Faber, 1981), 165.

Clement of Alexandria, *Stromata* 1.19, ANF 2.322.

Athanasius of Alexandria, *On the Incarnation*, trans. John Behr (Crestwood, NY: St. Vladimir's Seminary Press, 2014), 54.

Athanasius of Alexandria, *On the Incarnation*, 167.

Maximos the Confessor, *The Ascetic Life, the Four Centuries on Charity*, trans. Polycarp Sherwood, ACW 21 (New York: Newman Press, 1955), 1,10.

Maximos the Confessor, *The Ascetic Life*, 103–104, 109.

Chapter 7: "Pray unceasingly"

Maximos the Confessor, *The Ascetic Life*, 19.

Maximos the Confessor, *The Ascetic Life*, 114.

John Chrysostom, *Homilies on Matthew* 50; NPNF 1.10.313.

Sayings of the Desert Fathers; Thomas Merton, ed., *The Wisdom of the Desert* (New York: New Directions Publishing, 1960), 28–29.

Chapter 8: One, holy, catholic, and apostolic Church

Cyprian of Carthage, *The Unity of the Catholic Church*, 6; Cyprian of Carthage, *On the Church: Select Treatises*, trans. Allen Brent (Crestwood, NY: St. Vladimir's Seminary Press, 2006), 157.

Chapter 9: "We no longer knew whether we were in heaven or on earth"

Kallistos Ware, "Strange Yet Familiar: My Journey to the Orthodox Church," in *The Inner Kingdom: Volume I of the Collected Works of Kallistos Ware* (Crestwood, NY: St. Vladimir's Seminary Press, 2000), 3.

Chapter 11: Orthodoxy and the modern world

The Holy and Great Council of the Orthodox Church, "Relations of the Orthodox Church with the Rest of the Christian World," https://www.holycouncil.org/-/rest-of-christian-world.

Patriarch Bartholomew, "Address in Santa Barbara, California," November 8, 1997.

John Chryssavgis, ed., *On Earth as in Heaven: Ecological Vision and Initiatives of Ecumenical Patriarch Bartholomew* (Bronx, NY: Fordham University Press, 2012), 99.

Assembly of Canonical Orthodox Bishops of the United States of America, 2013 Assembly Statement on Marriage and Sexuality, http://www.assemblyofbishops.org/about/documents/2013 -assembly-statement-on-marriage-and-sexuality.

Further reading

Alfeyev, Hilarion. *The Mystery of Faith: An Introduction to the Teaching and Spirituality of the Orthodox Church*. London: Darton, Longman & Todd, 2002.

Alfeyev, Hilarion. *Orthodox Christianity*. 4 vols. Translated by Basil Bush. Crestwood, NY: St. Vladimir's Seminary Press, 2011–2017.

Angold, Michael, ed. *Eastern Christianity: The Cambridge History of Christianity, vol. 5*. Cambridge: Cambridge University Press, 2006.

Bartholomew, Patriarch of Constantinople. *Encountering the Mystery: Understanding Orthodox Christianity Today*. New York: Doubleday, 2008.

Behr, John. *The Formation of Christian Theology*. 2 vols. Crestwood, NY: St. Vladimir's Seminary Press, 2004.

Behr-Sigel, Elisabeth, and Kallistos Ware. *The Ordination of Women in the Orthodox Church*. Geneva: World Council of Churches, 2000.

Binns, John. *An Introduction to the Christian Orthodox Churches*. Cambridge: Cambridge University Press, 2002.

Bremer, Thomas. *Cross and Kremlin: A Brief History of the Orthodox Church in Russia*. Translated by Eric W. Gritsch. Grand Rapids, MI: Eerdmans, 2013.

Casiday, Augustine, ed. *The Orthodox Christian World*. London: Routledge, 2012.

Chadwick, Henry. *East and West: The Making of the Rift in the Church: From Apostolic Times until the Council of Florence*. Oxford: Oxford University Press, 2003.

Christensen, Michael, and Jeffery Wittung, eds. *Partakers of the Divine Nature: The History and Development of Deification in the Christian Traditions*. Grand Rapids, MI: Baker Academic Press, 2008.

Chryssavgis, John, ed. *Love, Sexuality and the Sacrament of Marriage*. Brookline, MA: Holy Cross Orthodox Press, 2005.

Chryssavgis, John, ed. *On Earth as in Heaven: Ecological Vision and Initiatives of Ecumenical Patriarch Bartholomew*. New York: Fordham University Press, 2011.

Chryssavgis, John, and Bruce Foltz, eds. *Toward an Ecology of Transfiguration: Orthodox Christian Perspectives on Environment, Nature, and Creation*. New York: Fordham University Press, 2013.

Crow, Gillian. *Metropolitan Anthony of Sourozh: Essential Writings*. Maryknoll, NY: Orbis Books, 2010.

Crow, Gillian. *Orthodoxy for Today*. Translated by Eric W. Gritsch. London: SPCK, 2008.

DeVille, Adam. *Orthodoxy and Roman Primacy*. Notre Dame, IN: University of Notre Dame Press, 2011.

Dvornik, Francis. *The Photian Schism: History and Legend*. Cambridge: Cambridge University Press, 1948.

Erickson, John. *Orthodox Christians in America: A Short History*. New York: Oxford University Press, 2007.

Erickson, John, and John Borelli, eds. *The Quest for Unity: Orthodox and Catholics in Dialogue*. Crestwood, NY: St. Vladimir's Seminary Press, 1996.

Evdokimov, Paul. *The Sacrament of Love*. Crestwood, NY: St. Vladimir's Seminary Press, 2011.

FitzGerald, Kyriaki Karidoyanes, ed. *Orthodox Women Speak*. Brookline, MA: Holy Cross Orthodox Press, 1999.

FitzGerald, Kyriaki Karidoyanes, ed. *Women Deacons in the Orthodox Church: Called to Holiness and Ministry*. Brookline, MA: Holy Cross Orthodox Press, 1998.

Ford, David, Mary Ford, and Alfred Siewers, eds. *Glory and Honor: Orthodox Christian Resources on Marriage*. Crestwood, NY: St. Vladimir's Seminary Press, 2016.

Geanakoplos, Deno John. *Constantinople and the West*. Madison: University of Wisconsin Press, 1989.

Geffert, Bryn, and Theofanis G. Stavrou. *Eastern Orthodox Christianity: The Essential Texts*. New Haven, CT: Yale University Press, 2016.

Gill, Joseph. *Byzantium and the Papacy 1198–1400*. New Brunswick, NJ: Rutgers University Press, 1979.

Gillet, Lev. *Orthodox Spirituality: An Outline of the Orthodox Ascetical and Mystical Tradition*. Crestwood, NY: St. Vladimir's Seminary Press, 1978.

Gillet, Lev. *The Year of Grace of the Lord*. Crestwood, NY: St. Vladimir's Seminary Press, 1980.

Hopko, Thomas, ed. *Women and the Priesthood*. Crestwood, NY: St. Vladimir's Seminary Press, 1999.

Hussey, J. M. *The Orthodox Church in the Byzantine Empire*. Oxford History of the Christian Church. Oxford: Clarendon Press, 1986.

Kasper, Walter, ed. *The Petrine Ministry: Catholics and Orthodox in Dialogue*. New York: Newman Press, 2006.

Kesich, Veselin. *Formation and Struggles: The Birth of the Church AD 33–200*. Crestwood, NY: St. Vladimir's Seminary Press, 2007.

Kolbaba, Tia. *Inventing Latin Heretics: Byzantines and the Filioque in the Ninth Century*. Kalamazoo, MI: Medieval Institute Publications, 2008.

L'Huillier, Peter. *The Church of the Ancient Councils: The Disciplinary Work of the First Four Ecumenical Councils*. Crestwood, NY: St. Vladimir's Seminary Press, 1996.

Limouris, Gennadios, ed. *The Place of the Woman in the Orthodox Church and the Question of the Ordination of Women*. Katerini, Greece: Tertios Publications, 1992.

Lossky, Vladimir. *The Mystical Theology of the Eastern Church*. Crestwood, NY: St. Vladimir's Seminary Press, 1976.

Lossky, Vladimir. *Orthodox Theology: An Introduction*. Crestwood, NY: St. Vladimir's Seminary Press, 2001.

Louth, Andrew. *Greek East and Latin West: The Church AD 681–1071*. The Church in History 3. Crestwood, NY: St. Vladimir's Seminary Press, 2007.

Louth, Andrew. *Introducing Eastern Orthodox Theology*. Downers Grove, IL: IVP Academic, 2013.

Louth, Andrew. *Modern Orthodox Thinkers: From the Philokalia to the Present*. Downers Grove, IL: IVP Academic, 2015.

Markides, Kyriacos. *The Mountain of Silence: A Search for Orthodox Spirituality*. New York: Doubleday, 2002.

Mathewes-Green, Frederica. *Welcome to the Orthodox Church: An Introduction to Eastern Christianity*. Orleans, MA: Paraclete Press, 2015.

McGuckin, John, ed. *The Encyclopedia of Eastern Orthodox Christianity*. 2 vols. Oxford: Wiley–Blackwell, 2011.

McGuckin, John, ed. *The Orthodox Church: Its History, Doctrine, and Spiritual Culture*. Oxford: Wiley–Blackwell, 2011.

McGuckin, John, ed. *Orthodox Monasticism Past and Present*. Piscataway, NJ: Gorgias Press, 2015.

McGuckin, John, ed. *The Path of Christianity: The First Thousand Years*. Downers Grove, IL: IVP Academic, 2017.

McGuckin, John, ed. *Standing in God's Holy Fire: The Byzantine Tradition*. Traditions of Christian Spirituality Series. New York: Orbis Books, 2001.

Meyendorff, John. *Byzantine Theology: Historical Trends and Doctrinal Themes*. New York: Fordham University Press, 1975.

Meyendorff, John. *Imperial Unity and Christian Divisions: The Church 450–680 AD*. The Church in History 2. Crestwood, NY: St. Vladimir's Seminary Press, 1989.

Meyendorff, John. *Marriage: An Orthodox Perspective*. Crestwood, NY: St. Vladimir's Seminary Press, 1975.

Meyendorff, John. *The Orthodox Church*. Crestwood, NY: St. Vladimir's Seminary Press, 1996.

Nichols, Aidan. *Light from the East: Authors and Themes in Orthodox Theology*. London: Sheed and Ward, 1995.

Nichols, Aidan. *Rome and the Eastern Churches*. Collegeville, PA: Liturgical Press, 1992.

Nicodemos of the Holy Mountain. *The Rudder (Pedalion) of the Metaphorical Ship of the One Holy Catholic and Apostolic Church of the Orthodox Christians, Explained by Apapius and Nicodemos*. Translated by D. Cummings. Chicago: Orthodox Christian Educational Society, 1957.

Ouspensky, Leonid. *Theology of the Icon*. 2 vols. Crestwood, NY: St. Vladimir's Seminary Press, 1978.

Papadakis, Aristeides. *The Christian East and the Rise of the Papacy*. The Church in History 4. Crestwood, NY: St. Vladimir's Seminary Press, 1994.

Parry, Ken, ed. *The Blackwell Companion to Eastern Christianity*. Oxford: Wiley–Blackwell, 2010.

Parry, Ken, David Melling, Dimitri Brady, Sidney Griffith, and John Healey, eds. *The Blackwell Dictionary of Eastern Christianity*. Oxford: Wiley–Blackwell, 1999.

Payton, James. *Light from the Christian East: An Introduction to the Orthodox Tradition*. Downers Grove, IL: IVP Academic, 2010.

Pelikan, Jaroslav. *The Christian Tradition 2: The Spirit of Eastern Christendom*. Chicago: University of Chicago Press, 1974.

Pentiuc, Eugen. *The Old Testament in Eastern Orthodox Tradition*. Oxford: Oxford University Press, 2014.

Plekon, Michael, ed. *Tradition Alive: On the Church and the Christian Life in Our Time: Readings from the Eastern Church*. New York: Rowman and Littlefield, 2003.

Rodopoulos, Panteleimon. *An Overview of Orthodox Canon Law*. Rollinsford, NH: Orthodox Research Institute, 2007.

Romanides, John. *An Outline of Orthodox Patristic Dogmatics*. Translated by George Dragas. Rollinsford, NH: Orthodox Research Institute, 2004.

Russell, Norman. *The Doctrine of Deification in the Greek Patristic Tradition*. Oxford: Oxford University Press, 2006.

Russell, Norman. *Fellow Workers with God: Orthodox Thinking on Theosis*. Crestwood, NY: St. Vladimir's Seminary Press, 2009.

Schmemann, Alexander. *The Eucharist: Sacrament of the Kingdom*. Crestwood, NY: St. Vladimir's Seminary Press, 1987.

Schmemann, Alexander. *For the Life of the World: Sacraments and Orthodoxy*. Crestwood, NY: St. Vladimir's Seminary Press, 1995.

Schmemann, Alexander. *Great Lent: Journey to Pascha*. Crestwood, NY: St. Vladimir's Seminary Press, 1990.

Schmemann, Alexander. *Historical Road of Eastern Orthodoxy*. Translated by Lydia Kesich. Crestwood, NY: St. Vladimir's Seminary Press, 1992.

Schmemann, Alexander. *Introduction to Liturgical Theology*. Crestwood, NY: St. Vladimir's Seminary Press, 1966.

Schmemann, Alexander. *Of Water and the Spirit: A Liturgical Study of Baptism*. Crestwood, NY: St. Vladimir's Seminary Press, 1997.

Schultz, Hans Joachim. *The Byzantine Liturgy: Symbolic Structure and Faith Expression*. New York: Pueblo Publishing Co., 1986.

Siecienski, A. Edward. *The Filioque: History of a Doctrinal Controversy*. Oxford: Oxford University Press, 2010.

Siecienski, A. Edward. *The Papacy and the Orthodox: Sources and History of a Debate*. Oxford: Oxford University Press, 2017.

Spidlik, Thomas. *Spirituality of the Christian East*. 2 vols. Translated by Anthony P. Gythiel. Kalamazoo, MI: Cistercian Studies, 1986–2005.

Staniloae, Dumitru. *Orthodox Spirituality: A Practical Guide for the Faithful and a Definitive Manual for the Scholar*. Translated by

Jerome Newville and Otilia Kloos. New Canaan, PA: St. Tikhon's Monastery Press, 2003.

Stormon, E. J., ed. *Towards the Healing of the Schism: The Sees of Rome and Constantinople*. Ecumenical Documents 3. New York: Paulist Press, 1987.

Stylianopoulos, Theodore. *Encouraged by the Scriptures: Essays on Scripture, Interpretation, and Life*. Brookline, MA: Holy Cross Orthodox Press, 2011.

Stylianopoulos, Theodore. *Sacred Text and Interpretation: Perspectives in Orthodox Biblical Studies*. Brookline, MA: Holy Cross Orthodox Press, 2007.

Taft, Robert. *The Byzantine Rite: A Short History*. Collegeville, PA: Liturgical Press, 1992.

Taft, Robert. *A History of the Liturgy of St. John Chrysostom*. 6 vols. Rome: Pontifical Oriental Institute, 1978–2008.

Valliere, Paul. *Modern Russian Theology: Bukharev, Soloviev, Bulgakov*. Grand Rapids, MI: Eerdmans, 2000.

Ware, Kallistos. *How Are We Saved?: The Understanding of Salvation in the Orthodox Tradition*. Minneapolis, MN: Light & Life Publishers, 1996.

Ware, Kallistos. *The Orthodox Church*. London: Penguin Press, 2015.

Ware, Kallistos. *The Orthodox Way*. Crestwood: St. Vladimir's Seminary Press, 1995.

Ware, Kallistos. *The Power of the Name: The Jesus Prayer in Orthodox Spirituality*. Oxford: SLG Press, 1974.

Wilken, Robert Louis. *The First Thousand Years: A Global History of Christianity*. New Haven, CT: Yale University Press, 2012.

Wilken, Robert Louis. *The Spirit of Early Christian Thought: Seeking the Face of God*. New Haven, CT: Yale University Press, 2003.

Wybrew, Hugh. *The Orthodox Liturgy: The Development of the Eucharistic Liturgy in the Byzantine Rite*. Crestwood, NY: St. Vladimir's Seminary Press, 1996.

Zizioulas, John. *Being as Communion: Studies in Personhood and the Church*. Crestwood, NY: St. Vladimir's Seminary Press, 1985.

Index